OBEDIENCE, STRUGGLE & REVOLT
Lectures on Theatre

Obedience, Struggle & Revolt

Lectures on Theatre

DAVID HARE

faber and faber

First published in 2005
by Faber and Faber Limited
3 Queen Square London WC1N 3AU
Published in the United States by Faber and Faber Inc.
an affiliate of Farrar, Straus and Giroux LLC, New York

Typeset by Country Setting, Kingsdown, Kent CT14 8ES
Printed in England by Mackays of Chatham plc,
Chatham, Kent

Some of these lectures have been published or excerpted by the
Guardian, *Areté*, the *Spectator* and Faber and Faber. We acknowledge
and thank these publications. All material is copyrighted.
'The Cave of Making', copyright © 1964 by W. H. Auden, and 'The
Truest Poetry is the Most Feigning', copyright © 1954 by W. H. Auden,
from *Collected Poems* by W. H. Auden; used by permission of
Random House, Inc., and Faber and Faber Limited.

A CIP record for this book
is available from the British Library

ISBN 0-571-22872-0

2 4 6 8 10 9 7 5 3 1

'All right, Zola is no Voltaire, none of us are Voltaires, but there are times in life when circumstances conspire to make the accusation that one is not Voltaire quite beside the point.'

Anton Chekhov

Contents

Introduction

It would take a great scholar of the English language to tell us when the word 'lecture' acquired such negative connotations. 'Don't lecture me!' 'I'm not taking a lecture from anyone.' 'It was more like a lecture than a play.' Look in the *Collins English Dictionary* and only one of the six given meanings is 'to reprimand at length'. But somehow the sixth has spilt over and infected the other five. What ought to be a purely descriptive word has come to carry heavy derogatory freight. Even a child knows to associate the word 'lecture' with adult superiority, long-windedness and boredom. Why?

Clearly, I'm biased. For reasons stated later in this collection, I have found it useful, for the last quarter century, to decorate the writing of plays and films with a kind of commentary – call it background murmuring, maybe, in the form of public address. More than anything, it has had the virtue of helping me examine my own ideas. The act of setting them down has clarified them, at least for me, if not for anyone else. I think I could best define a political writer as one who is likely to have an analysis as well as a view. By some quirk of temperament, I can't begin to write fiction unless I have more than a purely instinctive notion of what I am, at the out-set, intending to say. The finished play will then almost certainly turn out to bear as many differing interpretations as those of my fellow-dramatists who claim only to blunder about in the dark with no real idea either of where they're headed or of their reasons for writing. (Please reject absolutely the crazy Jonathan Miller suggestion that playwrights don't have intentions. Or that there's no need for directors to seek to discover them. They do. And there is.) But for me it's always been important to try and take some kind of aerial view – often as much about context as about content. That's also the reason to accept an occasional invitation to speak. Beyond my personal pleasure in the discipline of pursuing a line of argument for almost an hour lies my own preference as a member of an audience. Isn't it always more interesting to hear someone unmediated than it is to hear them clash in so-called debate?

To give you the idea: I've noticed, among my friends and acquaintances, that I am, for some reason, one of the few people who positively looks forward to the speeches at weddings. I'd go further. For me, they're the best part. Perhaps you may think me a cold fish when I admit that I have sometimes watched unmoved as the ring was slipped onto the finger, or as the first kiss was taken. (Priests always seem to be saying 'Not yet.') But I have never failed to feel a thrill of genuine anticipation when someone calls for silence and rolls out the magic words: 'Unaccustomed as I am to public speaking'. In one heart at least, the announcement does not cause a sinking. Far from it. Part of my interest is clearly professional. I am, after all, a playwright, and there is nothing more revealing of character than when a proud father or a jealous ex-lover acting as best man is forced to rise to their feet and 'offer a few words'. Yes, life *is* theatre, and the rituals which make private matters public are specially delicious. But I also love the prospect that, for once, somebody's spool is going to be allowed to run and run. Mark it down as optimism, but I cannot help feeling – at least before they speak – that the longer someone goes on, the more you are likely to learn.

It is the sheer rareness of uninterrupted speech which makes it so powerful, and which accounts for the recent, modest revival in the fortunes of the lecture. Like poetry, the lecture has come back into favour by its very dissimilarity from other more heavily promoted forms of communication. In Britain, we have long lived with the conventions of adversarial politics. The prevailing wisdom is that enlightenment may best be reached through argy-bargy. And yet in practice how infrequent it is, on television or radio, that the Socratic equivalent of men's tennis – massive slams hit back and forth from the baseline – actually illuminates anything at all. Panels are even worse. Taking part frustrates me as much as listening. What's the point? Why attend a forum in which as soon as anyone says anything interesting, somebody else has at once to be encouraged to interrupt, supposedly to generate conflict, but more often to dispel the energy of the previous speaker? Have you ever been present at a panel on which one person's perceptions *built* on another's? All too often, a panel degenerates into a marketplace for opportunistic grandstanding, with members rushing to take up positions, however irrational, which they hope are going to seem teenage-sulkier, wilder or more ingratiating than those of their fellow panel-members. If you could conceive of a formula least likely to inspire enthusiasm for the arts – non-practitioners would be invited to sit around on sofas speaking for thirty seconds and competitively show off about how superior they are to the artwork under discussion – then you would come up with *The Late Review*. If you wanted to make sure an hour would pass in which no serious thing could be said about politics, then you would invent *Question Time*.

Underlying this patronising conviction that no one person should be given the floor lies the idea that group discussion is more 'democratic' than an individual being licensed to hold forth. My experience is the opposite. The memorable parliamentary occasions have never involved the Leader of the Opposition biting hunks out of the Prime Minister's leg. They have happened when a politician with both insight and strong feeling – Robin Cook, say, or Barbara Castle – has been listened to by an audience, both in the chamber and outside, ready to interpret and weigh the exact impact and value both of what is being said and the manner of its delivery. When one person speaks and is encouraged to develop his or her ideas, then it is we, the audience, who provide the challenge. *We* provide the democracy. In each of our hearts and minds, we absorb, judge and come to our own conclusions. The dialectic is, thankfully, not between a group of equally ignorant people thrashing out a series of arbitrary subjects about which they know little and care less. It is between an informed individual who, we hope, has thought long and hard about their own area of specialisation, and an audience which is ready honestly to assess what the speaker has to say. Democracy, like everything else, thrives on preparation.

You might even say, then, that the lecture is attractive as a form precisely because a lecture so resembles a play. Critics love to reiterate the uninteresting idea that theatre depends on conflict. But actually it doesn't. It depends on engagement – engagement between the action on stage and the audience which attends. Screaming and shouting don't make a play. Nor do swordfights. Lectures and plays are alike in relying for their true vitality on the richness of the interaction between the performance itself and the thoughts and feelings created by the unspoken reaction in the room. Anyone who has had the luck to hear Robert Hughes talking about Goya or Stephen Pinker discoursing on the Darwinian interpretation of language will notice that in the fifteen minutes which is set aside for questions at the end, there is always an unusually high standard of interrogation. It is as if – hey! – the better the speaker, the deeper the response. A good lecture raises everybody's game. There is a contract. In return for the audience's presence, the guest is expected to have done a certain amount of work. The effort put into the thinking, is, in some wonderfully proportionate transaction of courtesy, rewarded by the concentration with which it is received.

So, for better or worse, collected together in *Obedience, Struggle & Revolt* are eight full-length lectures, which are mixed up with shorter pieces, some of which were conceived for memorial services and birthday parties, and some of which were intended for magazines. It takes me a long time to write a single lecture. To have managed even eight in twenty-five years counts as an unlikely accomplishment. Once I commit to a talk, usually well in advance of some reassuringly distant deadline – 'Oh don't worry,' says the host, with a Mephistophelean grin, 'November's months away' – then I face the prospect of giving up day after day of valuable playwriting time to wrestle again with the knowledge that a good lecture, were I ever to achieve such a thing, would be like a well-strung washing-line – taut from beginning to end. My progress in life, naturally, would have been much easier had I had been one of those gifted souls who can go before the public only with notes, or even more alarmingly, with nothing at all. (The very sight of some speakers' neat little postcards fills me with primitive jealousy.) But sadly I am condemned to read out every single word in the exact order in which I have set them down. You may say this method lacks spontaneity. So it does. But it also wastes less of the audience's time.

As to the subject matter, it should quickly become self-explanatory. One of the few common factors is that all these talks have covered ground of my own choosing. Whenever I have accepted a commission, be it to speak in Texas, in Wales, or in Westminster Abbey, it has always been left to me to decide whatever it is which is passing through my head. Nothing has been off limits. The invitation has always come from people who extend the gift of trust which is the *sine qua non* of intellectual curiosity and freedom. It was all the more depressing, therefore, to be approached in 2004 to give the Richard Dimbleby lecture for the BBC. For the first time in my life, I was being ordered in advance to declare both what my topic would be and how I intended to treat it. I passed up the opportunity. It seemed to me a fundamental transgression, a basic misunderstanding of what a lecture is meant to be. An invitation to speak is exactly that. It should not be an invitation to speak along approved lines. The very fact that an offer of forty-five minutes' airtime on BBC1 today comes preceded by an audition tells you a good deal of what you need to know about the prevailing cowardice of our great national broadcaster.

Most of these lectures relate in some way to the performing arts. At a certain point – I can date it exactly – I threw in my lot with the British theatre. It was a decision, and a conscious one at that. This was the place where I wanted to spend the greater part of my life. Inevitably, I have sometimes regretted it. But never for long. V. S. Naipaul has said that if he were a young man, he would no longer contemplate a life in literature, because the tradition he wanted to be part of has ceased to exist. Sean Penn has decided never to act on stage again, because he does not believe the American theatre any longer commands an audience which is interesting to play to. The work may be worthwhile, but the qualitative experience of presenting it is not. Well, perhaps. Inevitably, most of us in the older arts feel from time to time that we are spending our lives in what the film director Stephen Frears calls 'heroic retreat'. Our whole way of life may seem defensive, because we have a memory of values and forms which can sometimes appear to be of diminishing interest to the public at large. And yet, for all that, there is little profit indulging the self-pity of 'golden agery'. Anyway, it seems too easy.

As I make clear in the lecture which gives this book its title, my selfish intention as a young man was to try to put myself as quickly as possible in a place where I could live a less boring life. *Anything* to be less bored. (As my sister memorably remarked, the chief terror of getting pregnant in Bexhill-on-Sea was the danger that you might then never get out.) How can I not, therefore, feel a huge measure of gratitude to an art form whose central difficulties have been so thoroughly absorbing and demanding? Beyond that, I have thrived on the skill and friendship of many exceptional colleagues. Please consider the question of why the British theatre continues to attract, in even its most tangential functions – press office, lighting grid, prop room – many of the most thoughtful, intelligent and sheerly enjoyable people in the country. Something must be happening.

Obedience, Struggle & Revolt

This lecture was given in Melbourne, Australia, in October 2004, in the name of John Sumner, an Englishman who, from the 1950s onwards, did much to help establish repertory theatre in Victoria.

It's a peculiar thrill to be asked to give the second John Sumner lecture here in Melbourne. Most of you will be too young to understand that, for anyone of my age, our idea of your city was entirely shaped by the film of Neville Shute's novel *On the Beach*. The film appeared to recommend Melbourne on the interesting grounds that nuclear holocaust, like everything else, will arrive in Victoria three months late. Who can forget those familiar Melbourne residents, Ava Gardner, Gregory Peck and Fred Astaire – three natural-born Australians to the life – picking their way among the ponies and traps? Even in the late 1950s, Anthony Perkins was already having to deal with the incipient rebelliousness of the Australian female, which will one day make her a global by-word for wilful independence. Typically intransigent, the poor dear is refusing to take her suicide pill. 'I love you, I love you,' Perkins keeps saying, trying to push the damn thing down her throat. Oh yes, we got a very clear vision of what life in Melbourne was like.

In fact, my father had already told me a little. Dad had run away from school and from a family of bank managers in Ilford, Essex, first to be a jackeroo in New South Wales, and then to blow the cornet on a merchant ship. By the time of my birth, he had survived some hair-raising times in Atlantic convoys to become a purser with the P&O, taking out generations of colonial layabouts and cricketers on the last remaining islands of nineteenth-century British snobbery, for leisured journeys halfway across the world: deck quoits and dressing for dinner. There were eight chefs from Goa just to cook curry, and before Dad could reach down for his shoes, his servant Fernandez would already be on his knees to unlace them. We barely saw him until he was sixty. But we could tell from the generalised good humour with which Dad breezed back home, sun-tanned and carrying a thick roll of cash tied with a rubber band – a contrast, there, with our own style of life – that Australia was fun and that Bexhill, Sussex, was very definitely not.

And so indeed it proved on my own first visit. At the end of 1980, Jim Sharman got me to fly out so we could plan my half of a twin pair of plays which Sam Shepard and I were meant to write for the 1982 Adelaide Festival. It was a time at which I had despaired of ever writing a play again. I wanted to give myself a fright by abandoning my own protocol and accepting what remains only the second theatre commission of my life. I reckoned, in a cowardly way, that if I fell flat on my face, then I would at least fail twelve thousand miles away from the place where I lived. The newspapers reporting my humiliation would blow away down gutters far from my own. But nothing in my calculations prepared me for the blast of energy and high spirits which would send my mind spinning. Retiring for Christmas to a farm in Cooma with a distinguished relative from Canberra who was, at the time, *chef de cabinet* to the Prime Minister, Malcolm Fraser, I remarked how overwhelmed I had been by Sydney. Apart from anything else, in 1980, it was the most overtly and extravagantly gay city I had ever visited. 'Gay?' he said. 'What do you mean, gay?' 'Well,' I said, 'homosexual.' 'Homosexual?' he said. 'Sydney?' Then, after a moment's thought: 'I must tell the Prime Minister about this.'

It's important to stress that there was never a trace of condescension in my resolve to use Australia as a promising place in which to try and unblock myself. On the contrary. My play *Plenty* had been finished in 1978 and produced the same year at the National Theatre in London, with a commanding performance by Kate Nelligan, to a less than welcoming reaction from the British theatre critics. Bernard Levin, the excitable reviewer for the *Sunday Times*, had been moved to observe that he wished David Hare would just go away. Something in that phrase powerfully evokes the flavour of those days. Theatre seemed extraordinarily important. It aroused very strong feelings. We argued over it as if it were life itself. As a sceptical socialist whose youthful world view had been shaped by the Vietnam War abroad and by the corresponding failure of Harold Wilson's Labour governments at home,

I had reached a moment when I had little idea where either I or the world were heading. I was lost. *Plenty* was an epic of post-war disillusionment, the story of a young SOE agent flown into France in the 1940s, only later to become trapped in a backward-looking memory of courage from which, among the shabby accommodations of peace, she cannot escape. Ten years in the theatre had ended with my writing a play which dramatised the frustrations of someone who could not, however hard they tried, come to terms with a national loss of ideals. Fifteen years of being politically sentient had left the play's author with the definite foreboding that whatever tricks Western history now had up its sleeve, they were unlikely to be to his taste.

So, to be clear, I did not accept the job in Adelaide because I imagined the place to be some sort of plastic kiddy-slope on which I could once again pick up my skis. I wasn't *that* stupid. The first lesson of theatre was already plain: there is no such thing as an unimportant performance. To this day, I defy any writer or actor to watch the lights lower on any audience anywhere and not feel a cold hand twisting somewhere inside their bowels. I remember once walking onto a stage for a one-night charity performance and seeing the marks down the back of Michael Gambon's shirt: a shapely dark continent of sweat which corresponded to the rivers running down my own. 'Oh yes', Michael said, 'that never goes away.' ('Get through the door,' he advised. 'Close the door without fumbling. Say the first line correctly. Then say the next. Go on from there.') No, I agreed to write *A Map of the World* – for that was the name of the eventual play – solely and simply because I felt that if I did not write it now and for this place, I would never write again. It was, in my mind, as scary and dramatic as that. On the first night in Adelaide I entered the foyer to encounter the disturbing sight of the dramatic critics of the London *Guardian* and the London *Financial Times*, freshly belched out of a Qantas jumbo. They were talking contentedly together – grazing, really – as if their presence so far from their native killing fields were the most normal thing in the world. My illusion of freedom had been exactly that – an illusion. Lesson Two: in this business your enemies will follow you to the end of the earth.

You may, at this distance, find it hard to credit the measure of passion which moved us all and which marked out the ferocious theatrical arguments in the Britain of the 1970s. You might say, 'These were only plays, after all.' You might even notice that some of the hotly disputed titles which broke friendships and threatened theatres, which led to denunciations, rancour and lifelong accusations of betrayal, are those which have since been most completely forgotten. And yet, even so, it's impossible to think back to the years of my apprenticeship, both on the fringe and at the nascent National Theatre, without feeling afresh the vehemence, the violence, the almost impossibly strong convictions which led to a crazy heightening of language – 'Just go away!' – and to a near-hysterical sense of the importance of art which I have occasionally to remind myself is not a historical phenomenon.

These feelings came back to me recently when sitting at the cinema watching the film *Sylvia*. Few, sadly, will want to contradict me – unless of course the film-maker's mother happens to be in the room – when I say that the movie does not altogether succeed in capturing either the spirit or the essence of Sylvia Plath or of Ted Hughes. How could it? This kind of venture – the orthodox bio-pic – is, at best, a resolutely waxy version of entertainment. The purpose, in a Madame Tussaud's sort of way, is to emulate an original. But as few of the audience have ever encountered the original, the exercise often has a curiously pointless air. A work of art asks to be judged by a standard which has no meaning for the majority of its spectators. An actor is compelled, say, to scratch her ear, on no other grounds but that 'Oh, Sylvia always scratched her ear . . .' Who's in charge here? The artist or the subject? What's more, there is, inevitably, in any film about someone like Plath, a degree of speculation about things of which, by their nature, we can know nothing, and whose inauthentic portrayal any modestly sensitive audience is going to find deeply offensive. (I should declare an interest. I was at one stage, like everyone else, approached to write the screenplay – for Meg Ryan, as I remember – and refused on the grounds that I had no idea why Sylvia Plath put her head in the oven. I equally felt I had no moral right to reconstruct the dialogue and sentiments of a marriage to which I had no privileged access. *I wasn't there. I don't know.*)

However, even at what was inevitably a somewhat distanced and speculative evening, I was embarrassed spontaneously to be awash with tears. There is a section, perhaps twenty minutes in, when Sylvia and Ted inform each other that their intention, on leaving university, is to write the greatest poetry of the day – or some such nonsense. Clearly, it is hindsight which does lend the scene a certain sting. We know, after all, that Hughes did indeed go on to retrieve nature poetry from the immense influence of Wordsworth. Plath likewise succeeded, as she had hoped, in opening poetry up to whole new areas of feminine experience it had previously ignored or, worse, never even admitted to exist. But what made the scene overpowering, to me at least, so long after the events it described, was the sheer lunatic ambition, the awkward innocence of a time in which poets, from the unlikely base of provincial England in the late 1950s, set out not just to write the odd poem, but to change everything.

A further passage of autobiography may be excused if it proves how far this kind of resolution was from the inclinations of my own native temperament. I was born, as it happens, on the very day the Marshall Plan was announced. Even as my mother was confined in a Hastings nursing home, an American general was simultaneously announcing the details of his government's plan to set out on an act of massive international altruism: to provide the funds to save Europe from itself. From the perspective of the recent invasion of Iraq, it seems extraordinary to look back and remember a time, only fifty-seven years ago, when the preservation of Europe and the continuation of European values was considered the high priority of a non-selfish, non-imperial American government. Chance found me on the south coast of England, shut away into a semi-detached household, left behind with my mother and sister while my father sailed off to Aden, to Bombay and to Perth. The early years of my life passed in a suburban row of brick houses one mile from a pebble shore.

It amuses me now when politicians, usually from the very heart of the British Conservative party, emerge from time to time, and, in what is invariably a moment of complete electoral despair, call for a return to the values of the 1950s. Are they out of their heads? Only those of us who lived through that all-white decade can, in fact, recall just how stupefyingly uninteresting and conformist things were. For most of us, a return to the 1950s would represent a return only to repression, to hypocrisy and to a kind of willed, pervasive dullness which is the negation of life. Doris Lessing has argued that the seeds of the vitality of the 1960s were in fact sewn ten years earlier. The fifties, she says, were when it was fun to be alive. Maybe that was true in Earls Court. Elsewhere, no. From the early days of my secondary education, my dream was of getting away, of travelling the impossible sixty miles to the capital city. From the moment adult life first impinged on me, I had been able to make no sense of an emotional atmosphere which, I later discerned, had been created by an event which I had actually missed: namely, the Second World War. I was simply aware – who could fail to be? – that my parents' generation was fixated by a need for peace and quiet. 'Let's have a little peace', they kept saying. 'Can we please have some peace and quiet?'

My mother was a generous woman, sweet, kind-hearted, but fundamentally terrified of life. Her wish was to avoid it. At that time, it was not clear what experience it was which had bleached out the general ambition. Everyone above the age of thirty-five appeared to equate contentment with tranquillity. Their idea of perfect happiness was doing – and saying – nothing. Feeling nothing was better still. The flickering black and white box in the corner of the room arrived at just the right historical moment to render an already soporific atmosphere yet more passive. In the other half of our semi-detached lived a solicitor and his wife. She had perfectly mastered all the bourgeois rituals which we rather less convincingly sought to mimic. She knew the rules better than anyone. She even laid the table for breakfast the moment supper was finished. But by the time she took off her clothes on the wintry Bexhill beach and walked out to drown herself in the English Channel, it was evident that the generational tactic of peace-at-all-costs was not really yielding the promised dividend.

I was, from the start, a scholarship boy, the kind you find in every nineteenth-century novel, making his rather troubled way through society by brains and not by birth. I was sent first to a couple of Dickensian prep schools, staffed by ex-army misfits, one or two of whom disappeared mysteriously soon after they had reached a point of unendurable longing and finally whipped the towel from round the waist of some tiny object of love in the school showers. My mother's Scottish faith in the redeeming value of education propelled me onwards.

Another scholarship, another school: this time Lancing College, an Anglican foundation on the Sussex downs where inspired teachers pushed my horizons further and further back. I was ready. Culture began to act on me exactly as it is meant to, giving me the sense of worlds beyond my own – beyond the horrid prison of self – at last giving me access to some way of experiencing and interpreting that play between the familiar and the unfamiliar, the similar and the different, which is at the heart of all great artistic experience. Put it this way: you know it and you don't. Tony Hancock, Stendhal, Billie Holiday, Alexander Pope, Miles Davis, Federico Fellini, *Beyond the Fringe*: there was no guessing who or what would be flung at us next week by men who were trying to resolve the rich complexities of teaching a humanist syllabus in an avowedly religious school.

There it is. Art. The way out. The escape. You sense already that it's waiting, with its irresistible attractions and challenges, the stuff among which, it turns out, you will go on to spend your whole life. By the time I arrived at university I thought I knew it all. I had already begun to develop that sickening ease which follows on the ambiguous discovery that opinion comes cheap and achievement expensive. The drawback of all intellectual and social migration – of the journeys so many of us now make across class, across country and across culture – is that they engender contempt. Contempt becomes the poisonous carbon monoxide manufactured by the speed of your own progress. In some cases, it may be directed at those you have left behind or at the environment that produced you. It may be towards yourself: you may hate yourself for the fact that you want to advance. You may even direct your contempt at the ease with which talking any old rubbish will allow you a passport to a society in which ideas are not examined too closely. And contempt, above all, may become the most convenient way of disposing of old experience, so that you may once again press on to new.

You will, of course, detect in this description of my rootless youth a certain self-dislike. To be fair, I had already begun to notice that art, for so many people, could be a way of life, a style, a milieu, a means merely of not spending your future in retailing or in industry. By the time I reached Cambridge, the blazing vocational passion of Ted Hughes and Sylvia Plath was long out of fashion. Irony, worldliness and self-mockery were in. Jean-Luc Godard was our man, not Ingmar Bergman: dark glasses, not dark thoughts. People wanted to be cool. None of us liked to be caught out in the embarrassing position of being too high-flown, of taking ourselves too seriously. And yet if I am to speak a word in my own defence, if I am to try to understand the strange, jumpy figure in the beige rib-knit pullover and the white drainpipe jeans, smoking forty a day and grabbing every Marx Brothers film he could find, then I would say I had already begun the task of trying to resolve certain impossible confusions which still haunt me. You want the world to be different. You want injustice to be addressed. You want a social system which relieves the ubiquitous suffering of the poor. Why on earth do you imagine that theatre might be an effective, even an appropriate, way of achieving such things?

Oh yes, in the asking of this particular question lies a whole life-time, both of hope and experience, of bewilderment and of despair. What a weight we carry, those of us who elect not just to make stories, but to prefer that these stories should also convey purpose. We set off on a race, our legs already tied together by our convictions. We are the ridiculous people who insist, to universal scepticism, that not only must our fictions mean something: they must achieve something as well. Cambridge was no sooner finished than I was off, in the wake of May '68, to form a small touring company with my friend Tony Bicât, our simple, professed aim being to demonstrate to audiences everywhere the depth of the crisis within capitalism which would lead, within a few years, to its precipitate collapse. For some reason, we imagined an opening adaptation of Kafka's diaries would hasten that collapse. Pretty soon after, when a promised work failed to arrive from a teenage playwright, I was forced for the first time to lift up a typewriter onto my own knee, where it balanced as we sped along motorways from gig to gig. I began to imagine. In four days, I wrote an original one-act play, barely pausing for thought, let alone inspiration. By Monday morning, we were rehearsing. Without premeditation, the accidental transition from director to playwright had been made. It was only later, as I sat in horror watching the hideously inadequate result, curled up in the shaming gulf between what I had intended and what the audience all too plainly received, that in the full flush of failure I learnt what today we must call Lesson Three. You can will a theatre into existence. You cannot will a play.

You may fairly say that on that day – the day when I faced the humiliating wreckage of my own presumption – a longer journey began, and one which, in one sense, you may call redeeming. Balzac tells us that a young man or woman may choose only one of three paths – Obedience, Struggle or Revolt. Obedience, he says, is dull. Revolt is impossible. And Struggle is hazardous. If I was indeed, as I portray myself, a shallowly ambitious young man, then my good fortune, as a human being at least, was to be propelled by chance into a profession in which ambition counts for nothing at all. It is, as the Americans say, inoperative. The blank sheet of paper remains blank. Desire will not fill it, only imagination. And over that you have no control. It is given or it is not. Hard work is not necessarily rewarded. Drink and bad living are, thankfully, not punished. As time goes by, you may develop an instinct for the material which will suit you, to which the ungovernable voice inside you responds. You may even develop skills which make that voice sharper. But the act itself, the act of writing, remains as mysterious at the age of sixty as it was at sixteen. And its judgements are as harsh. No play exists in its description, in the ambition of what you would wish it to be. It exists only as it is, the thing, not the design.

It was Samuel Johnson who famously observed about the vagaries of human affection that you may demand kindness, but you cannot demand fondness. It is difficult to explain to anyone who has not experienced it the similar helplessness that attends the creation of any half-serious piece of writing. You wait, hoping the work may one day be uncovered – as if it were buried, pre-existent, and your task is simply to burrow it out from under the soil. My second life, my life as a writer, started back then in 1969 at the moment when I realised that I had just been introduced to a new companion at whose mercy I was going to spend the next thirty-five years. My creative self – the person inside me who would slowly go on to write twenty-two plays – was me and yet subtly not me. And, because of my companion's separate identity, an urgent dilemma would soon emerge. My desire was to use the theatre to argue for political change, and, at the start, to no other end. But early on it became obvious that the demands of what you would wish to accomplish politically cannot be so easily reconciled with what is artistically possible.

Lest this tension sounds too abstract, let me explain it in the simplest way. Imagine, if you will, the artistic programme which any vigorous and committed political writer would undertake if he or she were so empowered. He would make sure, for a start, only to address himself to the most important issues of the day. He would not waste his time writing about anything other than the gulf between the rich and the poor, or the ravaging of the planet by commerce because, of course, he would regard the examination of apparently lesser subjects as an obvious irrelevance. The medium this paragon would choose would certainly be television, because only by beaming his work into as many homes as possible could he be as effective as possible. And the preferred form of his storytelling would be strong, vigorous narrative. That favourite narcotic of the literary crowd, *nuance*, would be allowed to go hang because – again – the drama would be fashioned, above all, to be accessible. No member of the enormous audience would be able to mistake the author's purpose and meaning.

The fact that this unlikely dramatist I describe, adopting the strategy I describe, does not actually exist anywhere in the world tells us something about art, and about political art in particular. And yet it is a message which critics, directors and most especially progressive activists seem reluctant to receive. If you are known to be of a political turn of mind, then you will see in a producer's manner a distinct relief, because he believes, wrongly, that, for once, he is not having to deal with one of those impossible bastards who are stubbornly dependent on their personal muse. Dramatising history and the move-ment of society is mistakenly thought to be an activity more akin to journalism than to art. All the time, usually from the best possible motives, projects are suggested. The political playwright is there to be treated like a short-order cook. You are expected to be able to turn your hand to anything. What's more, it is implied that plays which directly correspond to events in the outside world will also be produced at a cost of less self-examin-ation, even less effort. If, like me, you are known to have written plays about the problems of the Middle East, the decline of the Church of England and the early progress

of the Chinese revolution, then you find yourself approached by artistic directors who seem confounded when
you explain that, regrettably, you will not be able to offer
similar entertainments on the history of the conflict in
Northern Ireland, the plight of the detainees in Guant-
ánamo and – one which often crops up – the struggle of
Shostakovich to survive as a composer of integrity in
Stalin's Russia.

No, however many times you say it, nobody seems to
grasp it. A snobbery is in play here, the snobbery of a
bookbound culture, especially in England, whereby works
about man's hopeless position in the universe are assumed
to be wrenched from inside the dramatist's furthest being,
whereas works which address themselves to social injustice are taken to operate on some lower level of suffering
and skill which will allow them to be knocked up, like
my miserable first one-act play, in a few days flat. It is
important – no – it is my whole purpose here to formulate what I, at some expense, have realised to be Lesson
Four, and by far the most important: the creation of a
great political play will demand exactly the same measure
of genius, torture and art as the creation of any other.
And maybe more. Yes, it is plain when we attend a performance of *Long Day's Journey into Night* that one of
the most gifted and anguished writers of the twentieth
century is offering us a matchless portrait of his own
family which cuts right down, deep into the bone of human
deceit. But when we see Brecht's *Galileo* or his *Mother
Courage*, what do we then think? Are we stupid enough to
imagine that the creation of two of the twentieth century's

most disturbing masterpieces on the subject of betrayal and selling out were not created at equal personal expense by someone who – let's put it politely – knew a little bit about betrayal and more than a little bit about selling out? What school of *Hello*-magazine-style criticism is it which insists that a play about your own family must be hard, but that a play about the intellectual disgrace of the Renaissance must be easy? Are Zola, Gorky, Hardy and Charles Dickens asking less of themselves in their socially aware writing than armchair stylists like Henry James and Vladimir Nabokov? Are they less refined? What crazy, stuck-up nonsense is this?

It is from this basic misunderstanding about the nature of political writing – the idea that it is different in its essential processes from any other kind of creative writing – that so many of the disputes of the 1970s flowed, and so much of the bitterness followed. At a time when Britain was in an alarming state of transition, angry positions were adopted. Playwrights were regarded as stubborn and unhelpful when they failed to produce the required works which would endorse those positions. Those who have chosen Revolt traditionally have little patience with those of us who favour Struggle. Many dramatists found themselves suddenly under attack from a utilitarian left which believed that everything, including art, could be judged only by how useful it was. It was good or bad according to whether it could, crudely, be marshalled to a cause. And at the same time some of us also came under equally lively fire from the right, this time, well . . . for no other reason than that we existed.

The right disliked me – no, that's too weak a word – the right loathed me because they claimed I was doing the very thing of which the left was meanwhile claiming I wasn't doing enough – turning the theatre from a place of harmless, corroborative entertainment into a boring dissenters' pulpit. Inevitably, one side wanted me to preach more; the other less.

Oh, they were high old times, not just for me, but for all of us. In recalling them it's hard not to feel a measure of rheumy-eyed nostalgia, the same old man's melancholy that overwhelmed me at that projection of *Sylvia*. Some impassioned feminists joined in, dismayed that at a moment when it was important to hear from a new batch of talented women playwrights, a conspicuous line of roles for women was, inconveniently, being written by a man and performed with relish by a series of great feminist actors. Shostakovich pointed out that 'The desire to avoid, at any cost, everything controversial can transform young composers into young old men.' Whatever else, that was never my problem. I was ageing from living controversy, not from avoiding it. My wounds stayed shockingly raw throughout the 1970s because I made myself vulnerable. I wanted to reconcile some kind of group impulse with the task of writing individual plays. Perhaps – who knows? – because of my fatherless upbringing, I loved the solidarity of a committed theatre movement. A sense of common purpose warmed me. And I loved being close to the life of an individual playhouse. I loved its feeling of family. I worked proudly as director with some of the most original playwrights of the day.

Nothing pleased me more than the sympathy of being part of a struggle for something more important and larger than my own work. So it was only at the end of that difficult decade – yes, when I came to Australia, clearly exhausted, and, I fear, diminished – that I accepted what more intelligent writers know from the start. I remember thinking: 'Oh, I see. I'm alone.'

From then on, life has been chillier but it has also been calmer. I long ago learned to expect nothing – neither friendly, upturned faces in the stalls, nor solidarity from anyone. I sit in my study writing at the same level of conviction and excitement as when I was young. *Stuff Happens,* a play this year about the diplomatic process leading up to the invasion of Iraq, absorbed and stretched me as completely as anything I wrote in my youth. Its performance thrilled me. And my views as a citizen are stronger than ever, my politics more resilient. But I am also aware that I am able to maintain fewer hopes of alliances, purposes or causes to which my plays can be shackled for more than a hundred yards of the hundred-mile road. Plays serve, and then they cease to serve. I have come to accept as an inevitable feature of the theatre that close partners like actors and directors are truthfully companions – pace-makers, if you like – who will walk with you along a path for a while before they decide that it's going to be more interesting to cut across that field over there. I have priorities of my own.

Theatre, I insisted earlier, is not journalism. The mistake is to imagine that simply because it can sometimes incorporate real-life material, so it can be judged by similar criteria. It is certainly true that the recent much-publicised flush of British drama on factual subjects is taken by many to be a response to the failures of the press. Audiences, at this time of global unease, urgently feel the need for a place where things can be put under sustained and serious scrutiny. They want the facts, but also they want the chance to look at the facts together, and in some depth. Everyone is aware that television and newspapers have decisively disillusioned us, in a way which seems beyond repair, by their trivial and partial coverage of seismic issues of war and peace. Front-page apologies in the more august East Coast newspapers, admitting professional gullibility, may show late stirrings of conscience, but they are hardly adequate to the laziness and stupidity of the mass American media in the last three years. The fact that journalism is too arrogant to recognise the crisis adds to the crisis. But even if it seems ungrateful to turn away both the attention and the praise which the medium of theatre has recently attracted by default, it is also important to point out to our new and clamorous public that theatre is not first and foremost a substitute for anything. It is itself, and what it does is unique.

You will expect me to end with some definition of that uniqueness. I shall try. Forgive me again a personal example. Two years ago I was approached by the distinguished director Max Stafford-Clark, whose Out of Joint company has somewhat specialised in the advocacy of what is now called verbatim theatre. The dialogue of real people is recorded and subsequently organised by a dramatist to make a play. (The process is akin to sculpture. You find the driftwood on the beach, but you carve the wood and paint it to make it art.) Max had the unlikely idea of a new project based on the recent history of the railways. Eager, as always, to sell me on the prospect, Max pointed out that, however terrible the result, the lucky playwright would nevertheless at the end be able to claim that they were the author of the best play ever written about the privatisation of British Rail. It would not, he said, be a crowded field.

My response, as you will by now have guessed, was to reply that I had no idea if I could write on so unlikely a topic, but I would at least be willing to enter a workshop, on condition that I was not committed in advance. For the first four days I sat trembling in some personal panic, going home each night in despair after listening to the testimony of those who had seen their favourite industry dismembered by an irresponsible Conservative government bent on ideological mayhem. The malicious replacement of a public-service ideal by a chaotic, private-service rip-off would make a powerful article. How on earth would it make a play? Then at the end of the week the bereaved mother of one of those killed in one of the train crashes attributable to the safety standards prevailing in the new privatised industry came to speak to us. Within a few minutes I began to feel a stirring, a disturbing subterranean wave of energy. In that moment something extraordinary occurred.

Flash forward now, please, to one year later and the eventual presentation of the finished work. In the intervening time, I have been repeatedly advised that although *The Permanent Way* is enjoying large audiences on its long regional tour of England, there is no real likelihood of any interest from abroad. It is a well-known fact, people tell me, that Americans, in particular, are indifferent to plays about mass transit. Imagine my astonishment, then, to find one of my closest American friends coming out of the play, which, among other things, portrays a group of people who have been radicalised into political action by the experience of losing the people they loved most. 'You didn't warn me,' he said, using a handkerchief to wipe away his tears. 'Why didn't you tell me? You never told me you'd written a play about Aids.'

Yes, to a New Yorker, the play had spoken powerfully because it addressed a subject about which he knew a great deal – the complex mixture of anger, confusion and steady purpose which awaits all human beings when they are forced to begin the agonising process of trying to draw a line between avoidable and unavoidable suffering. What more profound question can we ask? *Did this need to happen?* How many of the lives lost, either on the privatised railways or in the Aids epidemic in the Village of the 1980s and 90s, were the result of systemic failures, and how many would have been lost anyway? At the heart of *The Permanent Way* is an action group formed by the bereaved, who speak in a language which is completely familiar to anyone who has listened to those same groups which demanded the hearings to explain the reasons for the deaths in the Twin Towers. 'What they resent most,' says one bereaved mother, 'is that we're not the hysterical bereaved, we're the informed bereaved.' Both as a matter of personal healing *and* as a matter of justice – who would dare to distinguish between the two? – these groups have a lasting need to get to the heart of how and why their partners and relatives died. It's a way of honouring the dead. No, *The Permanent Way* is not about railways, any more than *Kes* is about a kestrel or *Moby Dick* about a whale. This is a play about grief.

To spell it out: the ingredient which makes all plays is metaphor. Journalism may be about only its ostensible subject and still be good. But of plays we ask something else, something more. Plays are indeed a world, and the trick of playwriting is to create density. Thickness is what you're after, solidity, substance, both to the painting of the people and to the filling-in of the themes. But thickness is no use without suggestiveness. Thus anyone who enters the theatre – of all forms – intending to use it primarily as a vehicle for self-expression is likely to come to a sticky end. Self-expression may be a by-product of telling stories, but it is not its purpose. Exemplary playwrights – think of Shakespeare and Chekhov – do not set off on their narratives with the intention of unburdening themselves about how difficult their own intimate relations have been. We may even say the greatest of writers are often marked out by a personal reticence which defies you to read their plays autobiographically and makes a fool of you when you try. Although any casual viewer of *Measure for Measure* or of *Uncle Vanya* will know at the end of their evening that they have been in the presence of a couple of writers who have rather more to offer, even in that narrow area of expertise, than the average mid-market agony aunt, nevertheless they will also know that confession has not been the purpose of the venture. Shakespeare may tell us things we need to know about human beings. But he does it through storytelling, not through self-revelation.

In a recent biography of Jerome Robbins, Deborah Jowitt makes this wonderful observation about a choreographer whose work was one of the glories of twentieth-century theatre. 'Atmosphere is crucial to his works and atmosphere is very hard to rehearse.' Atmosphere is also hard to describe, and lectures about theatre fail us if they do not remind us that words of description fall short of the experience itself. We know when theatre's working – when it's not solely about what it's about, but when it's about everything. That's when it works.

I Have a Go, Lady, I Have a Go

This was the inaugural John Osborne lecture, given at the Hay-on-Wye Literary Festival in June 2002 in the presence of his widow, Helen, and not far from the home on the Welsh borders where they spent the last years of their lives.

I don't see how any British playwright could be more honoured than to be asked to speak in public in memory of John Osborne. Just to invoke John's name and to recall the nature of his endeavour is to plug yourself straight into the main supply, the feeding house, the grid that makes our local culture spark and fizz. Here it comes again: the myth of the playwright who will seek to drive a straight line towards the heart of his or her own subject matter; the dramatist, educated in the playhouse not at the university, who will be neither academic and obscure on the one hand, nor stupid and populist on the other. Here they are once more, the playwrights who disdain pretension, false high-mindedness and didacticism, who won't talk down and who won't gussy up; these are the writers who don't want an art theatre or a theatre of snobs, who can't see a future in the etiolated antics of self-referential up-your-bum experimentalism, and yet who also refuse to set fallible audiences up – just people, after all – as the only or ultimate judges of their work, and who therefore aren't prepared to grovel and fawn in the cause of their amusement. Welcome instead to an ideal of theatre founded in recognition: spectators charged up by the presentation of their own lives, sitting in the dark, sometimes openly resentful, sometimes openly thrilled at the experience of confronting their own, often shameful, often dangerous feelings. Say the name 'John Osborne' and stick your fingers, as you longed to as a child, straight into the socket. Stick them in and sizzle.

It is an inevitable drawback of this, the first memorial lecture in John's name, that a period of seventy-three years after a writer's birth and of just eight after his early death offers perhaps the worst possible platform from which to give an intelligent account of a man's life and work. We are at the wrong distance. The German poet Rainer Maria Rilke called fame 'the sum of all misunderstandings which collects about a name'. Since it was John's great fortune to enjoy the most celebrated theatrical début of the twentieth century, so his misfortune has been consequently to attract some of its laziest and worst-aimed critical animus. There is a general feeling around that because John was never seen to be overly nervous of dishing it out, so there is no reason why he shouldn't also be given some. As in the case of Orson Welles, John's early acclaim has made the story of his life all too convenient a parable of squandered promise. What's the point of a myth if you can't de-bunk it? 'Misogynist', 'little Englander', 'embittered Edwardian', 'hopeless misanthrope', 'Garrick

club member' are a few of the cheerless epithets retrospec-
tively slung around in an effort to discredit the originality
of the man who lies in a grave in a Clun churchyard, on
the border between England and Wales.

No one can mistake the purpose underlying most of
the attempts to talk John down. Under the pious expressions of disappointment, the seen-it-all head-shaking
over a career begun in such high hope, lies a far more insidious, far more political project. Clearly, a fashionable
need exists, for reasons which we shall in a few minutes
try to explore, to attempt to deny the meaning of a
moment which has admittedly passed too easily into history. Behind the desire to belittle John and to belittle John's
work lies a much more urgent agenda. The plan, clearly,
is to challenge the myth of 1956 and what it is feared to
represent in British culture. This, let us remind ourselves,
was the establishment, by the force of a single play, written by a man who only one year earlier had been touring
as Freddy Eynsford Hill in a deadbeat production of
Pygmalion, of a principled new play venue in Sloane
Square. The Royal Court, as conceived by George Devine,
was to be a theatre committed to the uncommon notion,
to this day both revolutionary and banal, that at the
centre of all great dramatic adventure belongs the unpredictable, uncompromising figure of the living playwright.

'The hero has a sweet stall,' said Noël Coward, when,
at the age of fifty-seven, the old rogue came down from
his hilltop in Jamaica and for the first time admitted to
having read *Look Back in Anger*. 'I should like to know,
given his passion for invective, how the hero manages to

sell any sweets.' There is in that tone of oh-so-English put-down at least, mercifully, a simulacrum of style, the remains of a world-attitude, however feeble, however dated. But the trend-spotters of our own generation who, at the outset of the twenty-first century, line up eagerly to argue that the controversy raging around John's first performed play was all some kind of ghastly mistake, do not even pretend to any thoughtful view of why the work itself might once have triggered such astonishing contemporary passion. For them, the play's existence, and the reputation it carries of henceforward rooting most of what is outstanding in British fiction in the performing arts, are offence enough. Many people cannot bear the idea that a work of art can once have existed which conveyed so much power and effect. Their vision of living theatre is still best expressed in Robert Morley's timeless manifesto: 'All that English audiences need, deserve or want is me and Noël in terrible plays written by ourselves.'

In this modern atmosphere of spiteful revisionism – which now marks our politics as much as it does our culture; few people, God knows, wanting to be caught out looking remotely excited – it has sadly become necessary before speaking of any exceptional event to make clear what it is you are *not* saying before you go on to risk saying anything at all. When today I insist on the special qualities of *Look Back in Anger* and on its author's subsequent contribution to an interesting piece of English social history, then let me make clear that I am not thereby intending any implicit discourtesy to anyone else. To spell it out: I am not saying that, if you like that sort of thing, Christopher Fry was not a jolly good playwright; I am not saying that in her radical work at Stratford East Joan Littlewood was not a specific kind of English genius, gifted with a restless, fecund directorial inventiveness which this spectator has not seen matched since; I am not saying that Rodney Ackland did not, in the rush and hurry of new-wave agitation, get criminally overlooked in the late agonising years of his life; and I am not even saying that it is technically impossible to write a great play in which, for all I know, heroes and heroines burst with unbearable force through French windows, naked below the knee, bearing high-tensile tennis rackets, and with them, themes of shattering symbolic and spiritual importance. Given the right author, it may very well be. Stranger things go on in the name of entertainment. But I *am* insisting, however, that John did something almost unique. He reconnected the British theatre urgently to its audience, and he spread its influence way beyond its regular habitués and fans.

Again, in celebrating the genuine impact of this one play, it is essential to make clear that I am not describing something which we would today experience as a familiar piece of media contrivance. By chance, it was my own fate to end up as the author of one of the more publicised stage plays of the last fifty years when Sam Mendes asked me to adapt Schnitzler's scenes, *Reigen*, never intended for performance, and to re-set them in the present day, allowing only two actors to take the ten roles. When *Newsweek*, all smoky blues and flesh-tones, decided to forgo current events and pseudo-science and instead to splash Nicole Kidman in fishnet tights to herald the play's New York opening, then it was believed to be the first time that an American news magazine had thought a mere stage play worthy of its cover since the zenith of Tennessee Williams. But never for a moment did Sam, Nicole or I confuse a modern electronic sandstorm with either significance or reverberation. The three of us knew that *The Blue Room* was an innocent freak, mostly a freak of publicity. It was, in our eyes, a subtle and unsettling small-scale play, more tender than its reputation, which had somehow been picked up by the wind and taken for something it wasn't. Enemies of John Osborne like to pretend that the events surrounding his play were parallel: the first modern example, they say, of journalistic hype bringing a weight down on a play which it could not possibly carry.

The reply to this charge is best found in a performance of the play itself. When *Look Back in Anger* was well revived at the National Theatre only a few years ago, and unleashed from its original social context – for those of us who lived through them as infants, the memorably deadly early 1950s – then it seemed not at all the typically English play best known for initiating a supposed sea-change in English theatre. On the contrary – and most especially in the eyes of the foreigner sitting beside me – it seemed a defiantly foreign work; perhaps even a rogue, a sport, a one-off. 'Where did *this* one come from?' asked my neighbour. She could see no ancestry. She, like me, had been watching a Strindbergian account of a domestic relationship, which feels richer than

Strindberg for being layered with a knowledge of events outside the little room, for managing to imply the desolating movement of history, but which is also burning up emotionally with a most un-English intensity. For those of us still shaken by the events on stage, it seemed clearer than ever that John's trilogy of *Look Back in Anger*, *The Entertainer* and *Inadmissible Evidence* are not important for what they are said to have removed from the English stage – good taste, irony, deflection, lame jokes, and rigidly chewed upper lips – but revolutionary for what everyone now forgets they put in their place. I mean strong feeling.

'Yes, but what are you angry *about*?' It was, John said, the question he was most frequently asked – or rather, the second most frequent after, 'How much money have you made out of all this?' 'The English hate energy,' said one of the Royal Court's directors, Lindsay Anderson, who noted that no sooner had a new kind of drama begun at last to appear than the press rushed to give it the name 'kitchen sink', in an effort to patronise it, contain it and kill it with the easiest instrument to hand – the convenient English weapon of class. The legend tells us that when the curtain went up on that evening in May 1956, the audience gasped at the sight of an ironing board. More likely, they gasped at the sound of the words. For years, critics had been anticipating a poetic revival, and had turned their faces to the finer publishing houses of Bloomsbury for some stick-dry, crackle-breathed English poet to mimic the Elizabethans in the playhouse. In fact, when poetry did burst gloriously over the stage, it came, as always, from a direction which nobody was expecting:

from the mouth of a provincial trumpet-player, a malcontent, a cad.

(It is worth adding in parentheses that the second likely
reason for its exceptional impact was that *Look Back in
Anger* was the first English play for many decades to be
so clearly rooted in the pleasures of bed. Why else, as I
have argued before, was Kenneth Tynan so immediately
enthused by it? The play appeared at a moment when
approved theatre, as represented by Coward, Eliot and
J. B. Priestley, glowed with an erotic charge somewhat
less that a forty-watt bulb. Then John Osborne arrives,
childish or child-like according to your point of view,
but anyway blessed with a D. H. Lawrence-like conviction that people can't be known or understood except
through the act of love. The character of Helena – the
woman who affects to despise Jimmy Porter, but who
longs to sleep with him – is there to remind you that bed
will be the only crucible in which true feeling is revealed
and put to the test. My God, no wonder hackles went up,
stayed up, and have never really been taken down.)

The American pop historian Greil Marcus records
that when Elvis Presley went into the army, had his hair
cut and was posted to Germany, Marcus's first, unspoken
feeling was one of intense, shaming relief. To a boy
growing up in the US heartland Elvis rampant had been
an almost unbearable threat. Obviously, like everyone
else, you had to *say* you liked him – you had to follow
the script and *profess* to like him – but secretly you were
scared stiff. Elvis's gyrating hips, the insane sexuality and
throb of his music, the public example of someone

managing at once to be both so rebellious and so impossibly cool, seemed to bring home to the young Marcus everything that he himself was missing in his life, and implicitly therefore, in his character. If Elvis could be like this, then why couldn't you? You had no one to blame but yourself. The young knew that a gauntlet was being thrown down. And some of them also knew that they were both terrified and inadequate to pick it up. When the state got hold of Elvis and conscripted him, it was conscripting energy itself. When they proved that no one can survive for long in show business without being packaged into just one more nice American mother's boy – later, one more nice American mother's boy with the defining avoirdupois of the species – then Marcus pretended – again like everyone else – to be let down and cheated by his one-time hero. But inside, he felt other.

I have no doubt that, in a similar way, British resentment of *Look Back in Anger*, and recent attempts to rewrite its place in history, are, finally, resentment of vitality. One way or another, the bald can't wait for Samson to get a trim. Those expressions of disappointment about John's later work are, in fact, disguised expressions of gratitude that his challenge was not sustained. The eventual fallout between the critic who first championed the playwright's work and the playwright himself was both necessary and inevitable. A tide of gossip has always washed over Kenneth Tynan's ambivalent relationship with John – fan and fan-object – but gossip misses the point that their deepest disagreement was about theatre itself. In Tynan's eloquent admiration for what he called 'high-definition performance' you find what is fundamentally a worship of skill, of technique, of expertise, and implicitly therefore of success. In Osborne's values, you find a love of emotion, of high, true, uncensored feeling, of human weakness and therefore of failure. It was unlikely the two men were going to get on for very long. At the end of his life, Ken was left watching Shirley Maclaine and Marlene Dietrich. At the end of his, John was left reading *The Book of Common Prayer*.

'It is not the business of writers to accuse or to prosecute,' wrote the nineteenth century's greatest playwright. 'We have enough accusers, prosecutors and gendarmes without them.' This typically affable statement by Chekhov, on the surface so restful, so accommodating, so magnanimously fair, would make more sense to us and probably ring a good deal truer if we had not actually seen Chekhov's own plays, especially the younger ones. For all their fabulous likeability, these plays are, underneath, more unsparing of human failings than those of any dramatist I know. If, like the rest of us, you suffer from any hidden flaw which you might wish to conceal in your otherwise impeccable character, then the individual in all history with whom I would least recommend a relaxing weekend is a certain bearded Russian physician, anointed by his less discerning admirers with the word 'humane'. Your chances of driving away on Monday morning with your strategies of disguise intact I would rate as nil. It is precisely this quality, the ability to see through everyone, and most of all, to see through one's own pathetic fabrications, which marks out some of our most searching dramatists. (Such writers choose theatre because theatre is scrutiny.) And I suspect it is this quality – call it a certain ruthlessness of eye – which John's critics most distrust.

'It's hard,' suggests Christopher Hampton, in unlikely praise of Noël Coward, 'not to like a man who wrote, towards the end of his life, "I don't look back in anger, nor indeed in anything approaching mild rage; I rather look back with pleasure and amusement."' For my own part, when I think of Coward, I have to stick pins in my palms to remember not to despise him. Coward's great limitation as a playwright – and at once the source of his considerable comedy – is his determination to leave people as archetypes. He seals off their faults, letting them go by, as if they are just the traits people are born with, and about which they can do very little. 'Hey-ho,' as he would say. John's opposing instinct is to get things out in the open, to dig down and to look deep, to forgive no one, least of all himself. In his most popular work, *Private Lives*, Coward argues openly, and with the air of a man who believes that insouciance is a moral virtue, that it doesn't much matter what we do on earth because we're all going to die. It would be hard to imagine a philosophy more alien to John's. Underlying every word Osborne wrote is a rather different conviction. Because we are all going to die, it is therefore extremely important what we do now.

John's subject is, essentially, failure. John brings you news of what it is like not to succeed, to know you are not succeeding, either with yourself or with others – ever seen an Osborne hero with a dry brow? – and he does it in a medium in which the reality of failure is always more painful, more present than in any other. Why is John angry? Why are Bill Maitland, Archie Rice and Jimmy Porter angry? Because the chances of realising our dreams are so few, and the possibility is that, even so, we will miss our chances when they come. John is our poet laureate of flopsweat, of lost opportunity, of missed connections and of hidden dread, of what he himself calls 'the comfortless tragedy of isolated hearts'. John's plays are what you feel when you wake prickling in the dark: half-truth experienced as whole truth, intuition experienced as fact. John's characters, quivering, vibrating with life, have no clue how to put the nightmare away, how to chuck it, forget it, put a sock in it, repress it or even, for God's sake, how to talk the bloody thing to death. These are people to whom the fear always returns.

In retrospect, at what I earlier described as an inconvenient distance, I believe we can begin to see John as part of a rich generation of dramatic writers, whose prescience in the face of the arrival of a pervasive consumer society was to make a hugely romantic gesture of defiance in defence of the individual. Whether they were consciously political or not – and John, let's face it, could never make up his mind – these writers shared, in a broad way, a common analysis. In their view, the loss of an imperial role had sent the British into a period of painful self-ignorance. Boasting a ridiculous bomb they plainly could not use, and an international influence they plainly did not have, the leaders of our island race were behaving like embarrassing twits, while the people themselves appeared – in the public prints, at least – to be interested only in becoming paid-up members of the affluent society as fast as they possibly could. The novel in England, Doris Lessing honourably apart, had already turned its back on historical and social questions and gone into the dull slump of mindless solipsism from which it has never recovered. (To this day, you have to look to America – *Catch 22*, *The Catcher in the Rye*, *The Corrections* – for novels which reach out directly to influence people's lives; here, it is always going to be films, TV and theatre – *The Boys from the Blackstuff*, *Cathy Come Home*, *Look Back in Anger*.) And so it fell to the stage playwrights to mark out a vital patch of territory.

When they were alive, you would probably have felt that many things separated the sensibilities of writers as disparate as David Mercer, Dennis Potter and John Osborne. One, after all, was a painter and a Marxist; the second was a journalist and a Labour candidate; the third an actor and – well, a sort of faltering patriot. But as time passes, and what we lived through and just called 'life' is slowly seen to be history, so what these men – and yes, they were all men – had in common stands out more clearly. In each one of them you find a stubborn, ornery determination not to let themselves or other people be blanded into oblivion. What they have in common is what John himself called a delight in 'going too far'. Only by going too far, said John, could performed work begin to move into a place where unease in the audience becomes creative, where that funny meltdown happens when you no longer know what you think. When Dennis

Potter makes sure to alert us, in at least five of his plays, I reckon, to his own predilection for, and fascination with, prostitution; or when David Mercer, haunted by the examples of heroism in Eastern Europe, rails in flailing, drunken incoherence at the horror of remaining in the West, useless but alive; or when John, to the shock of all right-thinking people, judges it an autobiographical imperative to tell us of his desire to gob, like a passing bird, on his ex-wife's open coffin, then all three writers reveal a shared, underlying purpose. Their aim is always to hang on, to insist on what is dark, what is peculiar, what is disturbing – let me put it the way they would like me to put it: to hang on to what is *true* – in the face of what they fear to be the coming homogenisation of everything.

It will be obvious even to those of you not lucky enough to have met these three men in their prime that none of them was what you would describe as easy company. With each of them, I had at times variously difficult evenings. If we accept Flaubert's perfect definition of what one needs to get through life unscathed – 'To be stupid, selfish and have good health are the three requirements of happiness, though if stupidity is lacking, all is lost' – then we can see that for three such emotionally intelligent human beings, the battle for any easeful passage was probably lost before it was begun. And yet to someone of my upbringing, coming as I did from a quite different background and with quite different assumptions about what was happening in the 1960s, there was something almost bewilderingly masochistic about my seniors – writers perhaps ten or twenty years older – as if, sometimes, none of them were able to disentangle their profound and real hatred of what was happening to society with their much more shocking hatred of what was happening inside them. Who was the enemy here? Society or yourself? When my own play *Teeth 'n' Smiles* was presented at the Royal Court and widely greeted as the work of a new John Osborne – he'd done the music hall, I was doing rock 'n' roll – then I was flattered but confused. By quirk, I have as little sense of my own literary provenance as I do of the individual cow that provided my shoes, or the particular sheep that died for my supper. For me, deep influence is always unconscious. But it seemed axiomatic that I could have little in common with a writer whose priorities were, by then, so obviously different from my own.

Again, looking back, it is an odd paradox that my own gifted contemporaries – let's say, at least for the sake of argument, Howard Brenton, Howard Barker, Caryl Churchill, David Edgar and Trevor Griffiths – were greeted in the broadsheets as though they were the devil in hell, when they were, in person, so much more easygoing than their immediate predecessors. In Argentina, the Shakespeare comedy *Much Ado About Nothing* is given under the far snappier title *Much Noise, Few Nuts*. *Much Noise, Few Nuts* sums up pretty well the value of nearly all middle-aged critical reaction to the arrival of fresh life in the arts. When Bernard Levin used to launch his humourless, knotty philippics against a pack of playwrights who, he claimed, were intent on destroying civilisation itself (all served up in that atrociously contrived prose which more gullible parts of the *Times* readership used to mistake for style) then I would just laugh and wonder what would happen if Levin actually met any of my peers. Whatever personal torture and agony may have marked our private lives, we did not see it as part of our mission directly to display our individual souls on the stage. We felt we were putting just as much sweat, feeling and passion into our work, but it was clearly important to the exercise that romantic agony should not, for our purpose, necessarily show. (As William Empson put it, 'The careless ease always goes in last'). Whereas the generation before us were involved in a no-holds-barred defence of the individual, in which self-exposure, self-excoriation and even self-annihilation were regular ingredients, we, in our beginnings at least, were much more concerned to tell stories which might offer some equally passionate defence of the collective.

These were, I suppose, the only two sensible responses in the second half of the twentieth century to the sudden collapse of confidence in the West's sense of itself. You could either, as it were, regroup and insist that the duty of the writer was, at all times, to remind people that the human soul was deeper and darker than the countless numbing strategies of advertising and business – and of their outpost, Fleet Street – were planning to represent it. Or else you could assert, in the face of sometimes formidable evidence to the contrary, that the lot of human beings was still improvable. It seemed obvious to us: the pervasive feeling of national despair was not existential, but organisational. What we were lacking was not self-knowledge, but social justice. Whereas the collapse of the empire, the invention of the nuclear bomb and the brutality of Stalinism defined the thinking of people a little older than us, so the murderous war crimes of the Americans in Vietnam, the failure of social democracy under Harold Wilson and the continuing threat actually to use that terrible bomb marked our own. The achievement of a writer like Howard Brenton was to find unexpected comedy in the left's everyday passion for progress; the corresponding achievement of Trevor Griffiths was to compare the diamond-hard fervour of the past with the left's wavering accommodations of the present.

There is little, in this context, to add about my own plays, except to observe that I could not, for the life of me, work out why there were so few women on the stage that I had inherited. It seemed self-evident that an art form which sought to represent life could not be doing its job as long as it disallowed more or less half the human race from a position anywhere near the centre of the stage. I was aware, naturally, that most of my contemporaries had already abandoned the idea of the leading role. They saw it as invidious. Writers like Caryl Churchill chose to express exhilarating ideas through the movement of the group, and rarely through the articulation of a single individual: the Osborne tradition. Sometimes I designed plays for an ensemble of twenty-five, but when I also wrote the parts which were played by Kate Nelligan in *Knuckle* and in *Licking Hitler*, by Kate Nelligan and Meryl Streep in *Plenty*, by Helen Mirren in *Teeth 'n' Smiles*, by Irene Worth in *The Bay at Nice*, and later by Judi Dench in

Amy's View, then I was conscious of deliberately persisting in a practice which some people felt made nonsense of my politics. Why should one person have all the lines? I felt the contrary. Why should the contradictions of society – we live in contradiction, breathe it, swim in it – not be as powerfully expressed by one person as by many?

Clearly it remains a matter of historical record that the strategies of all our liveliest writers, whether of the left or of the right, were put in a new and unflattering perspective by the rise of a 1980s social movement which left many dramatists, and indeed the theatre itself, looking both weak and sanctimonious against an onset of energy to which it initially had little response. When global capitalism fired up its engines, freed up its markets, kicked up a gear and assumed its historic destiny of infinitely enriching the rich and further impoverishing the poor, then, for a while, culture stood on the kerb, like a vicar whose cassock has been splashed by a passing Maserati. None of us distinguished ourselves by the speed with which we responded to what was happening. A commercial producer requested me to cut the word 'capitalism'. 'Audiences,' he said 'don't like it.' 'OK,' I said, 'so what should I call it instead?' 'Oh,' he said, 'just call it life.'

We had all assumed for so long that the injustices of a particular system would somehow lead to some sort of reckoning, however crude, however violent, that everyone was rendered speechless when the system renewed itself from within. Mercer died suddenly, aged fifty-two – in Israel, as it happens, so he was buried in a British military cemetery, on the main road just outside Haifa. His last work was titled *No Limits to Love*. Potter started scouring his memories of the Forest of Dean, in search of terrain on which he might feel more at home. Just before his death, in a statement which summed up attitudes held in common by many writers of his age, he observed: 'For me, religion is not the bandage, it's the wound.' And John Osborne responded to the ubiquity of the present by retreating into the past. His volumes of theatrical memoir, which rank with Moss Hart's as the best ever written, fortify the myth of a golden age, a Utopia of memory in which George Devine is forever pacing the upper circle of the Royal Court, and in which girls, maybe a little squiffy, are forever waiting, with lipstick, bobs, short skirts and cigarettes in bars on the outer reaches of Chelsea or Manhattan.

Naturally, I cannot pretend that during these years of John's failing impact as a dramatist I felt wholly in tune with his predicaments. Other people's problems always look so much easier than your own. As a young man to whom the toolkit of politics was always ready in the garage to deal with random human breakdown, it seemed briefly obvious that if you based your defence of humanity on the personal pronoun, on the 'I' that is within us all, the 'I' that screams '*I* am unusual, *I* am valuable,' then you may soon find yourself more and more contemplating a painted view of a time and a place when that 'I' found perfect self-expression. Surely the word 'integrity' had to mean more than 'truth to myself'? John's comic fulminations against the arbitrary groupings that grew to attract his dislike no longer seemed to represent the strong, deep, true feeling he had once conveyed.

Instead he was forced back into a position which, finally, for most writers is both undignified and unproductive: the pretence that the past is always, necessarily, superior to the present. We had passed from passion to prejudice. Sometimes it appeared as if the moment of his own projectile heat had been so great, and so greatly defining, he could no longer find warmth anywhere else. In his last years, he appeared like the owner of a huge, peeling seaside villa, in which great parties had once been held. In his writing, he occasionally became careless of Duke Ellington's great injunction: 'Never forget: chords may be our love, but rhythm is our business.'

To be fair, life was not proving any easier for the rest of us. My favourite moment in Trotsky's writings comes when the great thinker demonstrates a fallible grasp of the American cultural scene by addressing his remarks to 'the workers and peasants of the South Bronx'. Those of us who had set out intending to address the workers and peasants of the British theatregoing community sometimes looked scarcely less silly. I certainly refused to cut the word 'capitalism' – always will refuse to cut it: capitalism *isn't* life – but even so, with Western society apparently charging off in an unforeseen direction, you would have had to have been one of Flaubert's happy idiots not to be aware of how hard it was to work in the traditional arts and not look ridiculous. In my world, it became expedient to say that it was no longer possible to write a play which would affect society's temperature, because society itself, the media and the West's love affair with mocking self-irony had reached a point where only decorative art could speak to large numbers. People wanted chopped sharks they could look at, not words they would actually have to think about. It was claimed that the moral arts were a bust. I thought this unlikely. If there was no modern *Look Back in Anger,* then the probable reason was that none of us were good enough to write it. For me, the aim of writing it, or rather, the aim of reproducing its effect, remains a timeless ideal.

Those who opposed John, and what John wished the British theatre to become, tend rightly to point out that nothing he stood for has come to pass. In support of their argument for his irrelevance, they assert that nowadays the playwright as truth-teller is, in their view, a dead duck. No dramatist, save Alan Ayckbourn, finds him- or herself anywhere near the centre of a decent-sized theatre's policy. Fifty years on, they are able triumphantly to boast that we have re-established a narcotic theatre of amiable revival, one which, hardly by coincidence, is run by career directors and bureaucrats, and in which the writers and actors hang on as the junior partners, hired and fired by their betters. These observers point with pride to the fact that the National Theatre has only sometimes been valued for its depiction of contemporary life. They prefer it in its most recent incarnation as a palace of operetta, and see no reason why a national theatre should not secede to a national Opera Comique. They are happy to celebrate the Royal Shakespeare Company's abandonment of any vestiges of their original motive for having a colony in London, namely the wish to do large-scale modern as well as classical work.

Above all, enemies of John are delighted that the most important new indigenous art form of the twentieth century, the single television play – to which John contributed and which was used to such effect, and with such reach, by writers like David Mercer and Dennis Potter – was first vandalised and then purposely eliminated by post-modernist hooligans at the BBC. In their short-sighted eagerness to stamp out individual voices, channel controllers managed, to their own considerable harm, to rob public service television of the only thing which made it different from other television enterprises. By a paradox, in fact, they destroyed the most effective argument they had for the licence fee. When the wounded soldier Robert Lawrence discharges himself from military hospital in Charles Wood's 1989 Falklands film *Tumbledown* and sets off alone in his wheelchair in a bid for freedom, then not only are you witnessing the final evolution of the Osborne hero – the man with, this time literally, half the back of his head falling out, raging against history, refusing comfort – but you are also present at the moment when the BBC resolves that henceforward, when you want distinctive drama, they will buy it for you from HBO.

And yet. For all that, for all the long years of compromise, it remains my conviction that something of John's great dream refuses to go away. Throughout my childhood, on the few occasions that he returned to our home, my father warned me to take notice that as a merchant seaman he was part of a dying profession. His experience had proved to him that large ocean liners would soon cease to plough their way to Australia, taking bullet-jawed military to India and white dinner-jacketed racists to the Far East. The world of mah-jong, mulligatawny and pink gin could not, he said, be with us for long. Dad implored me on no account to consider throwing away my life, as he feared he had his, by entering a trade with such an uncertain future. I obeyed. Instead I entered the British theatre. Now I find myself, it seems, still manning the poop deck of my own Peninsular & Orient. I can hear a few desultory games of quoits being played on deck – I hear scattered applause and the odd shout of encouragement – and somewhere in the bowels of the ship it sounds as if a few suburban parties in knee-length taffeta and penguin suits are still glassy-eyed, dancing to the keening melodies of fifty-year-old musicals. At the bow, the gulls circle, waiting for scraps. You may see things either way. Yes, theatre culture has been significantly weakened since Osborne's appearance. And yet it is also an astonishment, a miracle, a ravishment that living theatre has survived at all.

Seneca reminds us that death takes us piecemeal, not at a gulp. John's romantic attempt to go on throwing himself against the bars of the cage was not pretty, and, in my own view, it was also doomed. But, to his considerable credit, John went on writing, insisting on meaning, way beyond a point where the world thanked him for it. He did not, like his great contemporary Peter Brook, go into exile, where he would risk draining individual plays of any specific meaning or context to a point where each one was in danger of becoming the same play – a sort of universal hippy babbling which, at its worst, seems to convey nothing but fright of commitment. And nor did he, like Joan Littlewood, throw the whole boiling out of the window in understandable despair. For myself, I now identify with John, shamelessly. No question, as you get older, fiction gets harder. At my age, you spend a great deal more time feeling humiliated by the degree to which you are not Chekhov than you do celebrating the degree to which you are not Somerset Maugham.

'Don't touch shit even with gloves on,' wrote the Hungarian playwright, Ferenc Molnár. 'The gloves get shittier, the shit doesn't get any glovier.' The only help to us as we proceed, shitty and gloved, gloved and shitty, through life, is the example of those we have admired. I first met John in 1971 when we both had plays in the same season at the Royal Court. I sat on the steps with him in Sloane Square in the company of David Storey and E. A. Whitehead to have our photograph taken by the *Sunday Times*. John seemed shiningly confident. He had travelled only down the King's Road, but he appeared to have come from another world to my own. I was twenty-three. John was more expensively barbered than any man I had hitherto met and even his jacket was a work of art. I was in awe, unable to speak. A few words then, from me, would, I now realise, have been worth far more to him than the six thousand I am offering today. The silence between us was profound. We shook hands hopelessly and parted. I thought it was his job to say something. Only now do I understand it was mine.

Eulogy for John Osborne

A memorial service was held for John Osborne at St Giles-in-the-Fields in Covent Garden on 2 June 1995. Charac-teristically, John had ordered that a list be nailed to the door of the church excluding certain of his old enemies from attempts at entry. This is the text of my eulogy.

'I've an idea. Why don't we have a little game? Let's pretend that we're human beings and that we're actually alive. Just for a while. What do you say? Let's pretend we're human.'

It took the author's sudden death last Christmas Eve and his burial in a Shropshire churchyard, just a few miles from the blissful house he shared with his beloved Helen, to wake his own country into some kind of just appreciation of what they had lost. It is impossible to speak of John without using the word 'England'. He had, in some sense, made the word his own. Yet it is no secret that latterly John had imagined the local eclipse of fashion that is inevitable in his profession to be sharper and more hurtful than ever before. However, in the flood of heartfelt and often guilty appreciation which followed on his death, he would have been astonished to see publicly acknowledged what he most surely knew all along: that the world is full of people who feel strangely rebuked by those who dare to live far freer, more fearless, even more reckless lives than the ones we are able to lead ourselves. Of all human freedoms the most contentious is the freedom not to fear what people will think of you. It still shocks people when you claim the right to hate with the same openness with which you love. But even the stage carpenter at the Theatre Royal Brighton who liked regularly to greet the visit of each of John's plays with the words, 'Oh blimey, not you again' would have admitted that the man who wrote, 'Don't be afraid of being emotional. You won't die of it,' had all along been possessed of an enviable courage.

'It's deep honesty which distinguishes a gentleman,' he wrote on one occasion; 'he knows how to revel in life and have no expectations – and fear death at all times.' On another: 'I have been upbraided constantly for a crude, almost animal inability to dissemble.' Or, as his mother, the famous Nellie Beatrice, put it, after watching him act: 'Well, he certainly puts a lot into it. Poor kid.' Central to any understanding of John's extraordinary life – five marriages, twenty-one stage plays, and more flash clothes than anyone can count – is the striking disparity between his popular reputation as a snarling malcontent, the founding member of the Viper Gang Club, and the generous, free-spirited man that most of us in this church knew and loved. What he called his 'beholden duty to kick against the pricks' concealed from public view a man whom we all adored as an incomparable host, an endlessly witty and caring friend, and one of the best prospects for gossip and enchantment I have ever met in my life. He had, in Dirk Bogarde's happy phrase, a matchless gift for 'uncluttered friendship'. His postcards alone were worth living for. To a man writing from America to ask him the meaning of life, his typically courteous reply ran, in whole: 'Wish I could help you with the meaning of life. J.O.' To me, a colleague consoling him in some routine professional humiliation, he wrote from his beautiful home: 'Never mind. I lift my eyes to the blue remembered hills, and they call back: "Shove off."' To an Australian student, astonished to get an answer to his card saying he wanted to be a playwright: 'All I can say is trust your own judgement. Don't be discouraged by anyone. The only ally you will have is yourself.'

It is hardly surprising that right until the end of his life students and young people continued to write to him. The whole world knew that it was John who established the idea that it would be to the stage that people would look for some sort of recognisable portrait of their own lives. It would not be from this country's then-weedy novels, nor from its still-shallow and mendacious journalism that people would expect strong feeling or strong intelligence, but from its often-clumsy, untutored living theatre. Free from the highbrow pieties of the university on one side and from the crassness of what came to be called the media on the other, the theatre alone could celebrate John's approved qualities of joy and curiosity. It could also affront his deadly enemy, opinion. And for many years, ridiculously, this central

claim of John's, his ruling belief in the theatre's unique
eloquence, held and kept its authority. 'On that stage,' he
said, of the little space behind the proscenium arch at the
Royal Court Theatre, 'you can do anything.' John
knocked down the door and a whole generation of
playwrights came piling through, many of them not even
acknowledging him as they came, and a good half of
them not noticing that the vibrant tone of indignation
they could not wait to imitate was, in John's case,
achieved only through an equally formidable measure of
literary skill.

John was too sensible a man to make extravagant claims
for what he achieved. He knew better than anyone that
the so-called revolution attributed to him was on the surface only. The counter-revolutionary enemy was waiting,
preparing to send relentless waves of boulevard comedies,
stupid thrillers, and life-threatening musicals over the top,
in order to ensure that the authenticity and originality of
John's work would remain the exception rather than the
rule. Nobody understood the tackiness of the theatre
better than John. After all, he had played Hamlet on
Hayling Island, not so much, he said, as the Prince of
Denmark, as more like a leering milkman from Denmark
Hill. Yet behind him there remains the true legend of a
man who for some brief period burnished the theatre's
reputation with the dazzle of his rhetoric.

'I love him,' he wrote of Max Miller, 'because he embodied a kind of theatre I admire most. "Mary from the
Dairy" was an overture to the danger that [Max] might
go too far. Whenever anyone tells me that a scene or line

in a play of mine goes too far in some way, then I know my instinct has been functioning as it should. When such people tell you that a particular passage makes the audience uneasy or restless, then they seem (to me) as cautious and absurd as landladies and girls-who-won't.' There is in everything John writes a love for the texture of real life, a reminder of real pleasures and real pains. 'I never,' he wrote, in what I once claimed was his most characteristic statement, 'had lunch in Brighton without wanting to take a woman to bed in the afternoon.' When he heard that my own theatre company, Joint Stock, had gone on a mass outing to Epsom Races to research a play about Derby Day, his scorn was terrifying. He said when he was a young actor everyone he knew went to the Derby anyway, to enjoy it, not to bloody well research it.

It is fashionably said of John's work that he experienced a decline in the last twenty years of his life. There was nothing he resented more in later years than being asked what he was writing at the moment. Nobody, he said, asked an accountant whose accounts they were doing at the moment. Nor indeed did they ask: done any accounting lately? As he himself remarked, it is invariably those who have detested or distrusted your work from the outset who complain most vehemently of their sense of betrayed disappointment at your subsequent efforts. Yet in making this familiar observation critics ignore or take for granted the two exceptional, illuminating volumes of autobiography, which prove (if proof were needed) that his celebrated gift for analysing the shortcomings of others was as nothing to his forensic capacity for making comedy from his own failings. If he could be hard on others, he could be almost religiously brutal on himself. They also omit to mention what it was John declined from: a ten-year period, the last ten years of his great friend George Devine's life, in which he wrote *Look Back in Anger*, *The Entertainer*, *A Patriot for Me*, *Luther* and *Inadmissible Evidence*. Oh yes, John Osborne declined. He declined in the sense that an unparalleled, mid-century period of dramatic brilliance remained precisely that. Unparalleled.

'A real pro is a real man, all he needs is an old back-cloth behind him and he can hold them on his own for half an hour. He's like the general run of people, only he's a lot more like them than they are themselves, if you understand me.' The words are Billy Rice's, and yet they apply as much to John – more like us than we are ourselves, if you understand me – as to any music-hall comedian. 'Oh heavens, how I long for a little ordinary human enthusiasm. Just enthusiasm – that's all. I want to hear a warm, thrilling voice cry out Hallelujah! . . . Hallelujah! I'm alive!' It is a sad fact of John's life that in the country he loved one is judged either to be clever or to be passionate. There is in the condescension of many English people to one another an automatic assumption that the head and the heart are in some sort of opposition. If someone is clever, they are usually called cold. If they are emotional, they are usually called stupid. Nothing bewilders the English more than someone who exhibits great feeling and great intelligence. When, as in John's case, a person is abundantly gifted with both, the English response is to take in the washing and bolt the back door.

John Osborne devoted his life to trying to forge some sort of connection between the acuteness of his mind and the exceptional power of his heart. 'To be tentative was beyond me. It usually is.' That is why this Christian leaves behind him friends and enemies, detractors and admirers. A lifelong scourge of prigs and puritans, whether of the Right or of the Left, he took no hostages, expecting from other people the same unyielding, unflinching commitment to their own view of the truth which he took for granted in his own. Of all British playwrights of the twentieth century, he is the one who risked most. And, risking most, frequently offered the most rewards. For many of us life will never be quite the same without the sight of that fabulous whiskered grin, glimpsed from across the room. Then John heading towards us, fierce, passionate, and fun.

Why Fabulate?

Soon after appearing in the one-man show Via Dolorosa
*I wanted to try to answer the question raised by a young
Israeli actress mentioned in the play who abandons
acting – and forswears all fiction – on the grounds it is
'wrong'. Why, then, do so many of us now spend so much
of our time watching imitations of life? The lecture was
first given at the Royal Geographic Society in 1999, then
again in 2000, for English PEN International Writers'
Day at the Café Royal in London.*

> Be subtle, various, ornamental, clever,
> And do not listen to those critics ever
> Whose crude provincial gullets crave in books
> Plain cooking made still plainer by plain cooks.

I'll start, if I may, after Auden, with four chance remarks,
trawled from everyday reading, which have stuck like
burrs and scratched the surface of my brain. I emphasise
that I am paraphrasing two of them from memory. But
the sentiments have stayed with me precisely because
they were unforgettable.

In the *Guardian*, a British daily national newspaper,
Terry Eagleton, Professor of English Literature at Oxford

University, on being asked what books he most liked to read: 'Frankly, literature now bores me so much I'd rather watch men digging holes in the road.'

In the *Daily Telegraph*, another British newspaper – this time transcribed, not from memory – the academic Lisa Jardine, giving her reaction to a £6m BBC adaptation of Thackeray's novel *Vanity Fair*: 'I turned off after five minutes. I'm sick of period drama. I just thought, "Oh God, another one with bonnets." '

In the *New Yorker*, an American magazine, Bill Buford, its literary editor, introducing a fiction edition with the announcement that: 'The twentieth-century experiment of modernism is over. Pure narrative, story-telling is back.'

And finally, the response of Lord Redesdale, an English aristocrat on being told in the 1920s by his wife that *Tess of the D'Urbervilles*, which he had just finished, was not a true story, but written by one Thomas Hardy, 'What? Do you mean the damned sewer invented it?'

The first thing I hope you will notice about my choice of quotations is how bad-tempered they are. They share in common a definite sense of exhaustion – someone will inevitably call it *fin de siècle* – as if storytelling itself, its claims and its practices, had either tricked or exasperated the speaker to the point where they felt that a little blunt philistinism was the only possible response. In reply to that tone – which God knows enjoys popular currency these days – it is hard not to be equally forthright. To Terry Eagleton, for instance, it is difficult not to respond by admitting that his disillusion may, like, presumably, his own books, be sincere, densely argued and deeply felt. But if he is in good faith, he is probably unwise to go on occupying a prestigious post at a prominent university. Surely, if he is to follow his arguments to their natural end, he would be more honestly employed as Oxford's Arterial Professor of Road Digging while the Chair in Literature be yielded to someone who actually likes the stuff.

Of Lisa Jardine, it is hard not to ask what abysmal depths of professorial ignorance it was which made another respected teacher of literature think she could turn on an adaptation of *Vanity Fair* without being aware in advance that there was a sporting chance that the characters might be wearing the costumes of another era.

And to Bill Buford, it is important to point out that it is only a very narrowly based coterie of novelists who ever thought that narrative had been superseded. If Buford had looked up and out of the metropolitan chicken-run, he would have noticed that most people, after all, get the majority of their fiction from television, from films, from theatre and from the radio. In these forms, which can sometimes be more intimate with their audiences, narrative never went away. For all the supposed crisis in modern fiction, it is clear that humankind now enjoys more enactments of its own destinies than at any time in history. Television alone ensures that we fabulate, and we fabulate obsessively. But the majority of that fabulation goes on in genres, which are still, after a whole century of popular ascendancy, condescended to by literary editors in New York.

You will infer from my replies to these first three propositions that, temperamentally, a playwright has very little
patience with those people – be they critics or writers
themselves – who declare, in the middle of a lifetime spent
in the study of literature, that literature is in some way
failing in its duty to give them what they need. When the
modern academic adopts that deliberately crude tone,
then he draws attention not to inadequacies in literature,
but to inadequacies in him- or herself. It is rarely literature itself which has exhausted the critic. More likely, it is
his own obligation to write about it on a daily basis which
is actually getting him down. The complaints so many
critics make against literature are not true literary grievances. They are more often grievances of life-style. Anger at
the sustained difficulty of one's own job is not quite the
same as anger against the artwork itself. Modern criticism
would be considerably more interesting for the reader if
professors paused a second before next confusing the two.

An Oxford Professor of English who complains that
there is too much English about makes an obvious figure
of ridicule. The word for another professor who has seen
too many period adaptations on television is 'spoilt'. And
the editor who imagines that modernism has run amuck
through fiction is getting his fiction from unrepresenta-
tive sources. So it is surprisingly to the English aristocrat
that we must turn for the most probing and interesting
question raised among these four. 'What? Do you mean
the damned sewer invented it?'

It is impossible for somebody who has now spent
thirty years in the public profession of sewer – I dream

up invented stories and put them before the public – not to stop occasionally and ask himself not just why he is doing what he is doing, but what it is that he is actually doing. We are now used to the idea that the daily manufacture of fictionalised versions of our lives has unnoticeably become the essential background against which we conduct our own. You might say it is the defining mark of a modern civilisation that it finds itself *producing more stories*.

Each night, a near-majority of the population of Britain, in an action which plainly has no parallel in the previous history of our island race, sits down to watch actors simulate situations which the producers devoutly hope millions of people will recognise. What does it matter whether we call it art or not? Nightly, we expose ourselves to countless myths, both uniform and uniformed. Our representatives, those chosen from our tribe for their talent or for their beauty, pull on blue serge or green scrubs to appear before us as doctors, as policemen and as vets. But strangely, although this development is so singular and peculiar to our age, although we experience so many more of these artefacts than any large human group before us, we rarely pause to ask ourselves not just whether the consumption of endless parallel narratives to our own is necessary, but what on earth we think we are doing when we indulge in it, or rather when we indulge in it to such extraordinary excess.

People seem, in the twinkling of an eye, to have gone from finding everything in one book – the Bible, the Koran – to finding very little in very many. Towns in the mid-West of America which boast a religious bookshop and a pornographic bookshop, but absolutely nothing in between, are remarkable, thankfully, because they are now untypical of the world many of us inhabit. But what exactly is the reason for this multiplicity? Are we simply bored? Are we just lucky not to have to dig the fields? Does modern city life in countries at peace so lack passion and distinction that we can only find meaning by comparing our way of existence with others more dramatic and sensational? Does the restlessness with which we skip from one history to another signify the merits of an inquiring mind, or does it just imply an inability to settle on anything very much? Sportsmen, aviators, explorers read comics. It is we, the deskbound and the pavement-beaters, who prefer to search out subtler, more complex analogies. Is our aim, in short, merely to pass time which, in Beckett's phrase, would have passed anyway?

Some people will find the act of questioning the benefits of narrative culture impertinent and needless. The satisfaction they take in sitting alone with a novel, in listening to an opera or in going to the theatre is to them so ingrained, so obvious, that they barely stop to ask themselves why they think they are spending their time well. They would argue, rightly, that the twentieth century was marked out by two undoubtedly splendid developments. In the first place, art, in most of its forms, became available to the many rather than to the few. Thanks to the idea of universal education, to the influence of mass newspapers, to radio and to television, news of the pleasures of art reached more and more people.

But secondly, and, just as important, art itself reacted to the knowledge that it might be able to speak to a much wider audience.

Although it would be absurd to make any qualitative judgement about the grasp of twentieth-century literature, we can at least confidently say something about its reach. No longer was a Zola or a Dickens an isolated figure, eccentrically choosing to portray the lives of the poor rather than the rich. Now, and in particular through film and television, it was understood that the special potential of fiction might be to throw light where it had rarely been thrown before – on the daily hardships of the forgotten and the underprivileged. It was still possible, of course, at least in the first half of the twentieth century – though we may note much less in the second – to make major breakthroughs of technique: Joyce, Proust and Borges testify to that. But never forget that Hardy, Lawrence and Brecht made equally powerful breakthroughs of subject matter.

'Painting is dead, they tell me, but it's never concerned me,' said William de Kooning, who proved his point by going on painting long after his conscious mind was able to understand what his hand was doing. It is one of the most notable features of this age of artistic superproduction that just as the quantity of fiction produced has grown so alarmingly, so too has the number of observers ready, at the drop of a hat, to declare that all life has gone out of the activity. We no sooner open the cultural pages of a newspaper than some smart alec tells us that the novel, the theatre, the television play, the poem or the movie has died, but that somehow nobody except them has noticed. There is no more predictable nor more tedious way of filling up the pages of a broadsheet newspaper – and, interestingly, how those too have grown, in volume, if not in impact – than by giving them over to the obituary notice for some particular art form. There is no more glamorous way of opening a Book Fair than by heralding the Death of the Book.

'I had spent forty years reviewing plays,' said the recently retired British drama critic, Irving Wardle, 'and I didn't care if I never stepped inside a theatre again.' It is as if confronted with the sheer fertility of a supermarket, the easiest response is to smash up your trolley and start screaming that nothing in the shop is worth eating. But underneath this understandable feeling of helplessness – a helplessness which you may say oppresses us as much in politics as it does in culture – lies a deeper unease and one which does seem to have grown in the last part of the previous century. We cannot quite remember what virtue there is in telling made-up stories rather than in telling true ones.

The analogy with painting is, I think, a good one, because it was the introduction and growing popularity of photography which left painters wondering what they were going to do with their lives. If the job was no longer simply to serve as society's secretary, or as iconographer for its religion, then what was it? Plainly, portraying the Madonna was no longer enough. As news pictures acquired a clarity and immediacy which seemed to convey both urgent information and strong feeling to the public, painters began to wonder whether they were not, by infinitely complex means, doomed only to convey sensations which new methods of reproduction could deliver much more simply. The story of how painting found a role in the twentieth century is a particularly inspiring one, but the answer to its prosperity was indicated most clearly in Picasso's unexpected reply when he was told of the insult which a Royal Academician, Alfred Munnings, had paid him after looking at his work for the first time. 'Picasso,' Munnings said, 'can't paint a tree.' 'No,' said Picasso. 'He's right. I can't paint a tree. But I can paint the feeling you have when you look at a tree.'

It is this superior means of access to our inner sensations, this sense that the artist is inside us, knowing what we know but able to give it voice and shape, this gift, if you like, for expressing the inexpressible, which has offered the artist his traditional claim of superiority to the 'mere' documentarian. Music, of all the arts, we are told, is the highest because it is the nearest of them all to being at peace with its own irreducibility. It is, by definition, not a record of anything because it does not exist in relation to anything which can be adequately discussed or described. Music can only be experienced, and because it does not truck with the common currency of verbal concepts or ideas, it is generally held to be the closest to the sublime. But when literature and the performing arts seek the same status as music or pure dance, when they assert that they are, as you might say, something more than photographic, then they are forced to make a second and more contentious claim: namely that there is something called the 'higher truth' and that this higher truth can only be reached by the curious stratagem of lying.

From this artistic paradox – that by telling lies we reach the truth – an infinite variety of fun has been had by artists as various as Pirandello, Schnitzler and Luis Buñuel. If you can point to one prescient saying at the end of the nineteenth century which foretells all the artistic mayhem which will follow, then surely it is Oscar Wilde's ringing declaration in *The Importance of Being Earnest* that 'the truth is never pure, and rarely simple'. When Freud produced a theory which formalised the already growing conviction that we are all in only irregular touch with what goes on inside our own selves, then he cut the tape which allowed artists to pour onto a wonderfully irresponsible new field of play. Freud's bracing announcement that 'the ego is not master in his own house,' transformed the cultural world quite as much as it transformed the psychological. Not only were our characters unknowable. So were our motives. Surrealism thrived on the idea that we could not hope to distinguish the face from the mask, that dream might be as real to us as the real. There seemed no end to the good-natured sport that could be had by indulging the notion, in film and in written fiction, that human beings have the utmost difficulty getting to the heart of anything and – a very twentieth-century idea, this – that 'anything' may not in the long run turn out to have any heart at all.

But as the century drew to a close, you could feel people tire of the artist's too-easy get-out that there is no one truth, only yours or mine, and only at this moment and not necessarily for long. We had all heard too many dodgy biographical dramas, which had played fast and free with the facts of a person's real life, defended by their unscrupulous makers on the specious grounds that, 'No, well, it's not the literal truth of what happened, but it does express the higher, poetic truth of the thing.' No wonder the words 'higher, poetic' have become show-business code for 'inaccurate'.

Years ago, when a play of mine was performed in Holland, I asked my agent how it had gone. He replied that it had gone as well as a play possibly could in Holland. I asked him what he meant. 'Well,' he said, 'because of the remains of a Puritan tradition, people in Holland never really approve of plays, because plays are fiction, and what is fiction but lying?' It was my agent's reply which made me realise why the avant garde has always been so popular in that part of the world. It also brought back to me how in the days of popular stage nudity, you were guaranteed to see more actors scampering about buck-naked in Amsterdam than anywhere else in Europe. In the late sixties and seventies I was always fascinated to see that the Dutch took to the avant garde with the same ease and confidence with which English-speaking audiences took to musicals or soap opera. In particular, they responded to any kind of theatre which came close to performance art. They felt comfortable when the artist was willing to strip him- or herself down to become the subject of their own artwork. (It is no coincidence, by the way, that the television programme

Big Brother was originated in the Low Countries.) The
conventional playmaker or novelist, by contrast, uses
strategies intended not to reveal but to disguise. When
you walk naked in a public square, perhaps letting out an
unedited stream of consciousness at bystanders, then you
are doing something fundamentally honest. When, on
the other hand, you pretend to be someone you are not
in order to re-create events which never, in truth, happened, then you are conniving at what may, from one
point of view, be seen as a deliberate act of deceit.

'What, do you mean the damned sewer invented it?'

Those who have either missed or dismissed the cultural high jinks of the twentieth century may still think
that it is the test of any successful work to ask whether it
fools the reader or viewer into thinking it is true. They
may see Lord Redesdale's indignation as a sign of a job
well done. The noble lord may have been left feeling that
he had somehow been gulled, cheated into a sympathy
unworthily given, but Thomas Hardy would be justified
in congratulating himself on the skill with which he had
held a mirror up to nature. Eighty years on, however, it is
hard to imagine either such an innocent reader or indeed
such an innocent writer. If photography and the video
camera can claim now to provide a clearer, a less unreli-
able mirror than the individual artist, where, then, does
art belong?

The late twentieth century saw so many readers announcing that they preferred biography to fiction, and so
many television-watchers declaring that they preferred
the news – 'hard' news, 'real' news – to the contrivances

of drama, that you may suspect, as I do, that some shift was taking place in how the public wanted its cocktail, in exactly how many parts lies it was prepared to tolerate mixed up with how many parts truth. Although people were, mercifully, wearying of the fatuous cliché that there is more drama in ninety minutes of football than there is in the whole of Shakespeare, you sensed that this was probably because they were at last even more tired of soccer than they were of Elizabethan verse. But even so you could still feel people questioning what relation exactly the invented should have to the true.

For myself, I can only approach this difficult subject by taking examples from the world I know best. No play presented in London in the last few years was more impressive than Richard Norton-Taylor's remarkable re-creation of the Stephen Lawrence inquiry. Stephen Lawrence was an innocent black teenager, killed while standing at a bus stop. The murder of the eighteen-year-old Lawrence was the greatest British domestic scandal of recent years, if you count in the subsequent failure of the police to prosecute the gang of white racist youths who are alleged to have killed him. At the Tricycle Theatre in Kilburn you were nightly able to see extracts from the transcript of the judicial hearings. Norton-Taylor had done no more than to choose those incidents or testimonies which most interested or alarmed him. But in that act of editing, he laid before a live audience all the subtleties and intricacies of British racism, all its forms and gradations, with a clarity which I had never seen emulated by television, documentary or newspaper. The play seemed not just a rebuke to the British theatre for its drift towards less and less important subject matter: it also seemed to expose other forms by the sheer seriousness and intensity with which it was able to bring the theatre's special scrutiny to bear.

In an extraordinary decision, however, at the end of the year, the judges of the *Evening Standard* Drama Award decided that there had been no play in 1999 worthy of their prize. Having sat on a few award committees myself, I know that excruciating errors of judgement are endemic to the process. But in this case there was cause for special dismay. The only possible grounds on which the judges could have overlooked Norton-Taylor's outstanding work was because they did not think it was really a play. (They had also, by the way, rejected the year's second-best play on the grounds it was Australian.) It is true, of course, that the dialogue in *The Colour of Justice* was, as it were, 'found'. Norton-Taylor did not actually have to waste time in the tedious business of giving characters invented lines. But in his faultless act of organisation and selection, he had done precisely what an artist does. The audience knew they were watching a play, even if the *Evening Standard* didn't. By Picasso's great criterion, Norton-Taylor did not paint a tribunal of a racist crime. He painted the anger you feel when you look at a tribunal.

It was seeing that play that made me realise how lazy is the natural assumption that what we see on television, presented to us as fact, is in any true sense 'true'. When, in 1998, I wrote an account of a visit I had made to Israel and to the Palestinian Territory, then I became convinced that honour could only be done to complicated questions of faith and belief by dropping the familiar apparatus of playmaking and instead resolving to appear in my own play. As an outsider, a half-informed visitor, I despaired of writing fiction which relied on conventional scenes. Because I knew that English actors bearing machine guns and challenging each other at guard-posts, or wearing yarmalkas, or pressing their wrongly-proportioned bodies against the wire of refugee camps, would, almost by definition, introduce an element of falsity which would pollute the subject matter, so I determined to stand – yes, like a Dutch performance artist – making myself the vessel of the show in order better to direct people's attention to the material itself.

It was my contention that, in this case, when the subject of a work is so hotly contested, so open to argument, that the audience could best decide whether the witness were honest if the witness were willing to appear before them. To those who warned in advance that an acting debut was a foolhardy thing to undertake at the age of fifty-one, I could only quote Cocteau's injunction, which has been obeyed, in my lifetime, by all the artists I most respect: 'Whatever they criticise you for, intensify it.'

It is important to make clear that, in its writing, *Via Dolorosa* involved me in as much structural labour as any story with twenty-five actors and a dozen changing locations. It was a play like any other. It involved me in as much work. I tried scrupulously to convey the meaning of what the people I met had said to me. I even checked my version with many of them. But I also sought to order their words in the most dramatic and effective way possible. Their rhythms became mine. Although I intended a seemingly artless narrative which had me blundering ignorantly from one stirring encounter to the next – my own faithlessness contrasting with the passionate convictions of those I met – nevertheless the exact order of those encounters and some of the feelings they aroused in me did not in fact precisely represent the reality of my first journey to the area. The itinerary was rejigged. With the help of my director, Stephen Daldry, as much art went into this artlessness as would go into the making of a baroque altar. The play did not literally correspond to the letter of my experience. But it conveyed the spirit of that experience more faithfully than any 'mere' diary would have been able to.

The response to the work took me aback. People told me they had watched countless television documentaries, read countless articles, bought countless books, but that they had never felt close to the experience of the Middle East until they watched a play, a play which, for all its unusualness of form, nevertheless operated by all the conventional measures of fiction. Nothing could have made me happier than a comment from a news journalist: 'One leaves the performance with the conviction that one word can be worth a thousand pictures.'

As a result of this decision, as it were, to 'go Dutch', I am now frequently asked whether I'm giving up regular playwriting altogether. It's an irritating question, for not only does it miss the point that *Via Dolorosa* is indeed a play, but it also assumes that form is something which you apply to subject matter like paste, rather than something which grows from within it. *Via Dolorosa* was an attempt to escape from formula, not to impose a new one. Yes, it rejected old models. But it made no claim to be a new model. By standing alone on a stage, as Simon Callow rather unkindly put it, 'unprotected by an actor's shield of technique', it is true that I seemed able, on occasions, to convince the audience of an urgent sincerity which they had not always found in other plays I had written. I found a parallel in Blake Morrison's ability to move readers with his account of his relationship with his father in *When Did You Last See Your Father?* to a depth he could never have achieved had he laid on top of his memories the usual thin smear of fiction and called it a novel. If I could bottle the quality of the audience's reaction – their intense silences, their profound and mature consideration of the world I described – then I admit I would carry that bottle in my pocket for the rest of my life: a sort of playwright's elixir. But as soon as someone asked me, 'Oh, could you come and do Ireland now?' then it was clear there is no such thing in art as a formal solution that works more than once. 'If the novel is to survive,' said Carol Shields recently, 'it has to be subverted.' I would agree, but add that you can never subvert anything in the same way twice.

I have used the word 'mere' in inverted commas to speak of documentary and to speak of diary, for you will gather from what I am saying that I have respect for any artist who wants to drag art closer to reality, and whose inspiration is the wealth of the external universe. I have never wasted an evening in the theatre which put as high a priority on bringing knowledge as it did on bringing what the writer believes to be truth. How do we know anything unless we first look at some facts? Nothing has absorbed me more as a writer than taking apparently intractable subject matter – the Chinese Revolution, aid to the Third World, the prison system, the rigid rites and rituals of Alcoholics Anonymous, the far less rigid rights and rituals of the Anglican Church – and striving, often without success, to persuade people that something is more interesting than they realise. There are, after all, only three disciplines to which human beings can go for help in understanding their own predicaments: to art, to science and to religion. There is so much to know, and we have such short lives in order to learn, that I cannot understand any writer who, at some level, does not value curiosity over opinion, nor seek enlightenment over self-expression. What else will persuade the sated consumers that fiction can offer them something which the melodrama of football or the lassitude of magazines cannot?

You will, I hope, by now, see what I am arguing. The ceaseless reiterations of reality with which we are hourly bombarded, far from threatening the artist, to my mind offer him or her an increased and special opportunity. It is precisely because there are so very many stories being told that audiences need to be refreshed. Why fabulate? Because if we do not, everyone else will. We must fabulate because we all, as spectators, need to be brought up short and reminded that the lowest levels of fabulation, the formulaic levels which prevail everywhere, as much in half-baked novels as on half-baked television, do not, in fact, tell us very much about reality, or about ourselves. Bad storytelling, conventional storytelling, storytelling propelled by the doctrinal rules of UCLA screenwriting classes – Reel 10: hero confronts apparently insuperable problem; Reel 11: hero overcomes apparently insuperable problem – serves only to dull us. Such storytelling reduces the world and makes it less than it is. How much more desperately, then, we need our sense of wonder restored, given that so much in modern fabulation conspires to steal it away. Science, which effortlessly opens minds and exposes them to new ideas, will rob the arts of their audience if we are content to leave fiction clattering mindlessly along tracks it has traversed a thousand times before. The Dogme film-makers in Denmark who signed a manifesto forgoing the elaborate production values of American cinema have been mocked for their rigidity. The group appears to have disbanded after a handful of fascinating films. But who can deny their basic conviction that the very look of a Hollywood film has come to act as a kind of glaze which serves only to seal it off from the audience's feelings?

And let me be clear: not only do I look to leave the theatre or the television set knowing more, but most especially I hope to know more about now. The ignorant and foolish critic is the one who sneers that nothing dates faster than the up-to-date. A lifetime's experience of storytelling has convinced me that nothing is harder in the arts than to be contemporary. A majority of films and books could have been conceived any time in the last thirty years, because they are effectively reactions not to life itself but to other imitations of life. The deadly question 'Who are your influences?' presupposes of any writer that the primary source of their inspiration will not be what is happening now on the street but what has already happened between the covers of other books. But the film-makers who give fabulation a good name are those – like Mike Leigh, like Pedro Almodovar or like the great Iranian Majid Majidi – who make films which could only have been conceived in response to the contemporary world. The wash of period dramas of which Lisa Jardine complains would not, considered alone, be so lowering were these dramas not offered as a too-easy substitute for a once-thriving tradition of contemporary one-off plays on television. It is the ghost of what they have replaced which haunts us. 'Ah yes,' a television executive once smiled at me patronisingly. 'You write strongly-authored work, don't you?' 'Well what do you want?' I replied. 'Weakly-authored work?'

It was interesting during the Broadway run of *Via Dolorosa* – though not, significantly, during its run in the West End – to notice how much cultural commentary was provoked by the play's mix of the actual and the artificial. Controversialists fell on it like red meat. In particular the novelist Ellen Brockman was moved in the *New York Times* to argue that the play was part of a whole movement in the arts towards the real. In the face of so much representation of reality, the arts were, she argued, effectively throwing in the towel. In the Holocaust

Museum in Jerusalem I had noticed how much more powerful were the photographs of the camps than the terrible paintings and statues inspired by them. These artworks seemed somehow to diminish their subject matter, to achieve nothing except to insert an artist's presence gratuitously between people's unbearable suffering and our own reaction to it. From this section in the play, Brockman went on to conclude that my own cry of 'Give us the facts! It's the facts we want!' chimed in with a historical moment – a late twentieth-century feeling that art, which claims to interpret, in fact is only embellishing in a way that people now find unnecessary.

I was obviously pleased that someone had been stirred by my argument. But from the same analysis Brockman and I draw opposite conclusions. It may be true that we are breeding generations who will prefer to watch the security cameras in department stores rather than to go to the Royal Shakespeare Company. But it is interesting to note that, in television history, the fly-on-the-wall documentary which three years ago was all the rage is, in fact, now more or less extinct, while popular fictions like *EastEnders* and *Casualty* ride on regardless. The makers of these rightly admired and formidable programmes know something which the low-level documentarists did not: that the editing and organisation of reality is a genuine skill. In response to the ubiquity of the real, we need, not as Brockman argues, to abandon fiction, but, on the contrary, to make that fiction more original, more distinctive, to strive even harder to prove that only the greatest art comes near to matching the world's infinite suggestiveness. The enemy of art is not reality, but formula.

I began with Auden and I would like to end with him. In his last years, when his poetry was judged to be in decline, Auden wrote these startling lines, which apply as much to my profession today as they did to his then:

> After all, it's rather a privilege
> amid the affluent traffic
> to serve this unpopular art which cannot be turned
> into background noise for study
> or hung as a status trophy by rising executives
> cannot be 'done' like Venice
> or abridged like Tolstoy, but stubbornly insists
> upon being read or ignored.

In my youth, I remember being startled when the director Peter Brook remarked that he lived for the day when a theatre strike would inconvenience a community as much as a bus strike. Until people felt the same urgent need for drama that they do for a bus, drama was failing. That slightly ridiculous prospect ('I couldn't get to work this morning because there was no play last night') now has a whiff of sixties utopianism which seems as dated as William Morris or Craven A. At the turn of the century, out of the three million people who lived in Paris, half a million went once a week to a play, and twice that number went once a month. Edmond de Goncourt was able to observe, 'If you really want to be known in literature, you have to be on the stage, because the theatre is all the literature a lot of people know.' Now, a hundred years later, children no longer rush to the cinema at 10.30 on a Saturday morning to fall screaming with delight on the one film they will see all week. Don Quixote no longer leaps up from his seat, so carried away by the play that he takes out his sword to cut the puppets' strings. The day when art is felt to be needed is as far away as ever, not because we all produce too much, but because we all produce too much which is reductive. On the death of Dashiel Hammett, his colleague Raymond Chandler wrote this obituary for the father of the American detective story: '[Hammett] did over and over again what only the best writers can do at all. He wrote scenes that never seemed to have been written before.'

The world is not tired. Our reactions to the world are not tired. What becomes tired is the deadly habitude of our descriptions of that world. The artist exists only to externalise what we all do internally anyway. By making the descriptions new, we do not create alternative worlds. We remind people of the breathtaking beauty of the original.

A Defence of the New

This lecture came out of an invitation to speak at the Harry Ransom Center in Austin, Texas, in the autumn of 1996 to a foreign audience with an informed love of British theatre during a conference entitled 'Shouting in the Evening'. (The remark is attributed to the actor David Tomlinson's eight-year-old son, when asked what his father did for a living: 'He shouts in the evening.') The Center houses a manuscript collection by writers including Evelyn Waugh, Graham Greene and Tennessee Williams. On my return to London, the lecture was slightly adapted for the Cottesloe auditorium at the National Theatre.

If you ask me my all-time favourite playwriting story, then I think it would have to concern Bertolt Brecht in Hollywood. Shortly after his arrival in the United States, Brecht was convinced that he could develop a career as a screenwriter. With this aim in mind, he undertook a series of meetings with studio executives during which he, like any other common-or-garden writer, tried to pitch ideas for movies. Although his English was faltering, he was confident that he had a number of sure-fire titles and stories for films which the studio would find itself unable to resist. To that end, he pitched one scenario – understandably, his own personal favourite – under the unforgettable title *Boy Meets Girl, So What?* It seems to me wholly to Brecht's credit that he nursed a continuing grievance that Hollywood seemed never to appreciate his most inspired ideas.

In some sort of comparable dilemma, I have found myself searching for a suitable name for this talk today, which I am choosing to present under the admittedly rather feeble title 'A Defence of the New'. I would probably not have put this talk together at all, had I not been invited three months ago by an American university to give what diplomats like to call a *tour d'horizon*. It is some tribute to the power that the subject continues to hold over the imagination that you can find four hundred people in Austin, Texas, willing to give up their weekend to a remarkably lively and informed discussion of a theatre culture four thousand miles removed from their own.

Like most playwrights, I have a fear of pontificating on something called 'The State of the Theatre'. I have argued before that this is something which people who actually work in the theatre are almost uniquely disqualified from doing. It was amusing to read the well-known English director Deborah Warner in the paper recently saying that she felt that the exchange between British and American theatre was now dead, that there was no more profit to be had from English eyes turning westwards. Whatever benefit had accrued from the regular exchange of ideas between New York and London was now over. Instead, she confidently declared that the British theatre belonged primarily in Europe where it would be able to develop a much more profound creative rapport. The next day you realised that the reason she had advanced this fascinating thesis was, simply, that she'd just been offered a job in Paris.

This is something to which, frankly, all theatre artists are prone. Not only do we rationalise our own particular choices – 'I feel the musical theatre is terribly important,' says someone who has just agreed to write the lyrics for the latest inane mega-musical – but also we use talks about 'The State of the Theatre' as a subtle vehicle for talks about what we really mean – namely 'The State of Our Own Work'. The same Deborah Warner also recently announced that the straight play in the orthodox playhouse was dead. It was no longer possible to do interesting work in theatre buildings. The future lay instead in found spaces like disused factories or abandoned warehouses which, once adapted, somehow gave theatre a presence and freshness which was no longer possible in the outdated Victorian caverns or the modish concrete bunkers in which plays were more usually presented. Again, one's only response to this ludicrous generalisation is to say that just because Deborah Warner no longer wants to work in theatre buildings, that does not actually mean that all theatre buildings are therefore facing permanent extinction. I trust I am as egotistical as the next theatre artist, but even I can see that there are dangers in projecting one's own state of mind onto the theatre at large and feeling thereby entitled to draw universal conclusions. If nothing else, theatre is various. Good work, we can say confidently, will still be done in good theatres, even if, sadly, Deborah is not there to do it.

It is also the powerful sense that the roots of your own theatrical decisions are, at bottom, mysterious which makes pronouncements from a platform like this one so arbitrary, and, unless one is careful, so actively misleading. In my own lifetime I have bought all sorts of different artistic prescriptions. At one time or another, I have believed that all theatres should be touring theatres; I have believed that all plays should be presented by ensembles; I have believed that my own work should be presented on the ends of piers; and even, at my most demented, I have become convinced that directors should be altogether eliminated from the process of making theatre. Yet each time I have fallen sway to a particular belief, I have held to it with what felt like absolute sincerity, because – I realised afterwards – it suited whatever artistic instincts were gripping me at the time.

Crucially, I have also known that these instincts have been formed in ways over which I have not had conscious control. Asked rationally to defend or explain the paths a playwright has taken over the years, most can only reply that theatre does not work like that. Plays are not entirely constructed according to plan. Admittedly, for me, it has always been vital to work out a play's political underpinnings. The most difficult character to get right in a play is yourself. Who are you? What do you believe? From what standpoint are you telling the story? A writer of my inclination will always be fascinated to discover how the performance of their work then chimes with the temper of the times. (Thus, after the uncertainty of opening, the value of performance lies as much in what it reveals about the audience as it does about the play.) But even so, a perfectly valid answer to many of the questions you may be asked about particular characters and particular scenes is an unapologetic, 'Because I felt like it.' Without the employment of that response and its fraternal twin, 'Because it seemed right,' how do we explain the baffling choices the playwright makes in *Hamlet*? In *King Lear*? In *The Winter's Tale*?

It is hard, therefore, for me to take entirely as they are intended those little manifestos which visionary playwrights produce entitled *Fifty Paths to a New Theatre* or *Twenty-Seven Rules for the Redefinition of Drama*. Although they are often set out like route maps, Baedekers, if you like, for other theatre artists to follow on the way to some utopian view of what theatre might become, they seem to me to serve much better as genuine sources of illumination as to how we should read or experience their author's own work. Supposedly describing a real world which exists outside the playwright's head, they seem more often to shine light inside it. Although Brecht, for example, thinks that his theoretical writings in some way tally with the progress of his plays in the theatre, even he, the great German theorist, finally throws up his hands at the end of his life and begs his interpreters to trust the plays themselves, and not to be misled, as many have been, by his own writings about them. If you examine them at all closely, these writings are often both internally contradictory and wildly at variance with the meanings audiences discern at the plays' actual performances. As someone who has recently adapted *Mother Courage*, I can only tell you the play does not say what Brecht thinks it does. He intends it as a parable of the profit motive: audiences, rightly or wrongly, now experience it as being about war's inexhaustible appetite for death.

For me, therefore, as for most playwrights, a single play is worth a thousand speeches. In my view, George Bernard Shaw, offered one million dollars by an American newspaper to impart one final message to the world from his actual deathbed, was wise to decline the money. Apart, presumably, from not quite knowing what to do with the million when he had only a few hours to live, the author of *Heartbreak House* and *Pygmalion* knew that by limiting himself to the words he actually used – 'There is nothing more to be said' – Shaw was admitting that the moment had come even for him to suspend the voluminous commentary which he had hitherto kept up on the subject of his own work.

And yet. Plainly, there was a purpose in my accepting an invitation to speak in the US at the Harry Ransom Center, a library which, for one reason or another, boasts a more comprehensive collection of modern playwrights' manuscripts than the British Library. I found that the act of speaking abroad forced me to face truths about my own profession which had lately been troubling me. It was impossible for me to talk without confronting some genuine unease of my own. In England, to our shame, we no longer have serious theatre magazines, perhaps because, like all weakened species, we no longer wish to be seen to disagree in public. Standards of professional criticism and commentary in the British theatre are notoriously low. Newspaper reviewing is lodged in the reactionary hands of men and women who have no nose for genuine excitement, whose instinct is always to support the safe, the formulaic and the gestural, and who seem, worst of all, to have mislaid the you-would-think-job-defining capacity for explicating the ideas of a play. Is there a single critic writing today with the skill or conviction to relate the essential meaning of a play to human experience outside a theatre? But whatever the absence of outside analysis, I am sure that I am not alone in coming to the feeling that things inside the London theatre are at some sort of crossroads – and, for once, not simply one of my own projection.

In a recent opinion poll, when asked what it was that made them proud to be British, over sixty per cent of respondents replied that they could not think of a damn thing. You may feel that this answer says more about the national temperament than it does about the actual state of the country. In my lifetime Britain has burst with many things, but pride is not one of them. But for years now when people have talked about the things the British do well, then the two invariables in such lists have tended to be the state of our gardens and the state of our drama. It has become something of a commonplace to say that in these two fields – the arrangement of hydrangeas and the production of modern plays – the British are some kind of world champions. No tourist guide is complete without mention of the glories of English acting and the satisfactions of the West End. So it was alarming last year,

1996, when approached by foreign visitors about what they must not miss while they were over, sometimes to find myself pausing fatally before answering. For the first time in my life, in answer to that familiar question 'What should I see?' on occasions I hesitated and, yes, for some time even racked my brains.

In reporting this, I do not mean to suggest that there were not all sorts of excellent presentations which are a tribute to a rich and unusual tradition. Although the London commercial theatre seemed to be going through one of its rockier periods, lately offering some – let's say – indecisively aimed work, nevertheless in the subsidised area you could still go and find your faith rewarded. You could let Penelope Wilton break your heart as the mother in O'Neill's unfailing masterpiece *Long Day's Journey into Night*; you could rub your eyes to ensure that you were not hallucinating, but that it was indeed the great Paul Scofield standing there in front of you in Ibsen's *John Gabriel Borkman*, his hair slightly dusty as if sprayed with Christmas snow, but speaking in the same tremulant vibrato which thirty years ago impelled you into the heart of King Lear; you could see the incomparable Irene Worth at the Almeida, playing George Sand, and still able at eighty with a single gesture to summon up an entire vanished culture; you could catch an excellent *Tartuffe*, a fine *Mary Stuart*, a young *Glass Menagerie*, a sizzling *Virginia Woolf*. You could hear Marianne Faithful sing *Falling in Love Again* better than Marlene Dietrich; and Mandy Patinkin sing Sondheim better than . . . well, better than anyone. The lazy libel that British theatre is primarily verbal and careless of visual potential could be casually disproved at a dozen different shows by the work of a new crop of outstanding young designers. Yet even as you attended this work, you were aware that this season was, in its spirit, timeless. It was often terrific, but only in a way in which the London theatre might have been terrific had the Royal Court never happened, or had the theatre not seemed once, briefly, likely to become the defining English art form of the century. What we were facing was a season, however rich, which was just one more season like any other.

Before anyone hastens to tell us we are spoilt – that here, after all, was a feast if only we knew it – then I must explain that it was not for the regular satisfactions of the classical repertoire that some of us entered the theatre in the late sixties. It is easy to mock the impulse which first attracted my generation to the idea of stage performance. We were clear-eyed. We liked theatre because we thought we could use it. To us, the theatre existed for mainly political purposes, to try to dramatise, more tellingly than any piece of reportage, what we took to be the irrevocable decline of our culture. We accepted, as we now accept, that British theatre would always resemble a supermarket. On one aisle would be all the silly comedies, with their saucy flashes of thigh and their strangely neutered young men; on another, the thrillers, with their wobbly sets and astonishing coincidences; over here you could find the endless, slightly numbed revolution of the same Shakespeare plays (Stratford-on-Avon, with its declamatory style and shameless sucking-up to audiences, we held in particular horror); over there, you could seek out the big-melody musicals and the star vehicles. But my own trip to the supermarket was justified, you might say it was made sense of, by one special section, the section which perhaps served as the store's loss leader, the area which vindicated the entire effort and made it meaning-ful: the corner where the new plays were on show. The purpose of the whole complex ecology of British theatre – its drama schools, its publishing firms, its repertory com-panies, its cross-pollination with pantomime, with music hall, with television and with film – was, as far as I was concerned, in order that new works might be produced which truly played to the current concerns and interests of the audience that attended them. The theatre should not just reflect life. It should represent it.

It is important when talking in general terms about this kind of expectation to point out that the author of the most successful play in this genre never claimed that the essential character of the British theatre had been changed by its reception. John Osborne was in himself far too clever and also, with his record as an actor in rep, far too knowledgeable about British theatrical taste, ever to put forward such a view. Although *Look Back in Anger* would have imitators, although it would provide much-needed encouragement to a hundred other writers who looked at what John had done and instantly *took heart*, he knew that the battle to make the British theatre serious, to make it grown-up, would have to be carried on every day and against overwhelming odds for the rest of his life. If this was to be a revolution, it could only be a Maoist one. The forces of reaction were powerful. Critics seized gratefully on John Whiting's cheesy phrasemaking about the Royal Court – 'I have seen its big heart but what worries me is its tiny head' – in the hope that by repeating his slander often enough they might make it come true.

Anyone who has worked in the theatre for any length of time comes to understand that advances in taste sometimes turn out to be temporary. Theatrical life has always more resembled Stendhal's description of the battle of Waterloo – foggy chaos interrupted by sudden bursts of apparently random activity – than it does the generals' own view of battle as steady, purposeful and always in a forward direction. In a recent article in *The Spectator* the critic Milton Shulman, who had never much liked plays not set in Eaton Square, gloated openly about the failure of the Court to change the face of British theatre. Pointing out that the despised and unfashionable writers of the fifties, Terence Rattigan and Noël Coward, were the two heroes who now received the most regular and loving revivals from the young, he was able to assert that the influence of John and his friends had been considerably less than they had hoped. Conveniently ignoring the fact of Osborne's own admiration for Coward, and Rattigan's equal respect for many of the playwrights who followed him – somewhere he is quoted as saying he would like to have been Joe Orton, but did not dare – Shulman committed the vulgar error of attributing to John a would-be influence that he himself never claimed. (At the end of his life, John told me in despair that he believed it would have made no difference if he had never lived.) But if you could lay aside the ugliness of Shulman's impulses and his vengeful eagerness to stamp on the importance of something which had never called itself important, he did however seem to point to some greater truth: that if you examine the overall repertory of plays which are currently performed, in London at least, then it seems in its essential mix remarkably little changed from the middlebrow, unambitious selection which attracted so much contempt even forty years ago.

It is not just the plays which have not changed much. Nor, truly, has the audience. If one kind of post-war energy went into the aim at Sloane Square of changing what was seen, another equally significant movement pioneered by Joan Littlewood was intent on changing who saw it. The early part of my own theatrical life was, typically, dedicated to taking violently contemporary plays to army camps, villages, prisons, school floors, and all sorts of similar places where theatre was not usually seen, in order to introduce a new audience to the special pleasures of the medium. Yet, as the years have gone by, I think I may also be typical in coming to see that the artistic benefits of playhouses which enable me to say infinitely complex and sometimes delicate things may outweigh the satis-factions of what were often, again, only temporary gains in the constituency for theatre. Like many playwrights, I have come to admire my audience more as I have got older. I like the fact that they turn up. Whoever they are, and wherever they come from, I also value their concen-tration when they are there.

The danger in admitting this is that of course I begin to sound defensive. But I do not know anyone who has endured the fashionable onslaught against theatre in the last ten years who has not occasionally sounded if not defensive, then at least a little bewildered and rueful. In Britain at least this has not been an easy period. The once-serious practice of arts commentary has been adjourned to a sleazy motel room, where newspaper and magazine writers have been conducting an unreciprocated love affair with pop culture. Supposedly upmarket journalists have been heard making fools of themselves, like granny at the disco shrieking 'Give it to me baby' at every leather-clad American stud who happens to pass. Meanwhile, followers of live rather than mechanically reproduced performance have correspondingly been told they are irrelevant and out of touch.

In Britain, it has long been expected that the priests of literary culture will look down on the performing arts. They imagine films and plays vulgar and in some way slightly suspect, when compared with the rarefied business of writing novels and poems. But lately the snobs have made common cause with the populists. The great, revolutionary studies of popular taste pioneered by Raymond Williams and by Richard Hoggart have been misappropriated by less scrupulous writers into an easy method of vindicating market-driven laziness and stupidity. What Williams and Hoggart intended as a means of refreshing culture has been twisted instead into an approach aimed at confining it. All argument must now freeze in the face of the paralysing formula: 'If it's popular, it must be good / If it isn't popular, it must be elitist.' Theatre's value has been persistently questioned by a generation of graduate writers who regard the form as too difficult and too cumbersome to bother themselves with. (It achieves its effects too slowly. It goes too deep.) At the same time, the theatre's industrial confidence has suffered a definite internal decline, perhaps from realising that the fight to convince governments of the value of art can never finally be won. If we are to receive subsidy, then it must be fought anew every week, wasting an energy which everyone is longing to spend more profitably on the actual production of plays on the stage.

Last year, at an event at the Royal Society of Literature, when challenged by the audience about all the problems of under-funding in the regions and the dangers to what used to be a vigorous national network of repertory companies producing a whole range of classics and new plays, Tom Stoppard attracted some hostility from the audience by describing himself as 'complacent'. Although he was himself personally nostalgic for those days when as a young man he had eagerly attended every performance at the Bristol Old Vic, he recognised that the world had changed, and in the new environment of television, video, satellite and internet he was content for his own children to come upon theatre more gradually, as one option only in their much more frenzied lives, and one in which they had the right either to be interested or not, as they chose. Theatre as a form had no special or automatic right to survive and prosper.

By speaking in this way, Stoppard not surprisingly out-raged older people in the audience whose own formative memories were of intense, even obsessive theatregoing, and who felt that the present generation was somehow missing out. Yet when my own turn came to speak, I had no problem backing Tom up. I knew already from reading *Arcadia* that Tom, in his writing at least, takes what one might call a rather relaxed view of human history. But even so, I found myself, to equal hostility, agreeing with him in his refusal, in Faust's great phrase, 'to bid the moment to remain'. After all, in one sense, nothing had changed. The work of first-rate playwrights still palpably had a unique power to communicate. I said we could all think of examples. We had all seen individual plays which spoke straight to our hearts. If there were no longer *enough* examples to generate the kind of special passion which, say, marked out the mid-fifties in recent history, it was most certainly not the culture's fault. It was our own.

Since I was the author of a recent trilogy of plays about three British institutions (the Church, the Law and the State), observing the audience had taught me that whatever the aesthetic judgement on these plays might be – whether they were in fact any good or not – there was, in the quality of the audience's attention and the extra-ordinary variety of their response, a palpable wish in the public at large to have a place where they could go to see the currency of present-day life set before them, and, in intention at least, given some sort of shape. The thirst, unarguably, was there. To judge from our audiences, the throats of the young seemed to be quite as parched as those of my own generation. I contended that if we fail to satisfy that thirst, then we have no one but ourselves to blame. If the theatre appears, as it often does, to be drifting from the centre of many people's interest, then the likely reason is that not enough good writers are writing good enough plays.

Obviously, this is a hard view, and you might well object that it is a highly privileged one. In Britain, after all, it is impossible to disentangle the subjects of culture and education, and it is only the occasional appearance of an exceptional playwright like Shelagh Delaney or, more recently, the brilliant Andrea Dunbar – who wrote *The Arbour* and *Rita, Sue and Bob Too* in exercise books from the Bradford council estate where she lived – which reminds you of the massive untapped creative potential among people who would never normally think of going to the theatre, let alone writing a play. You cannot, in England, begin to imagine the number of people who are simply never given the means to dream of any other life but the one to which they appear to be condemned by circumstance. For all the superficial changes in the British class system, the single greatest scandal in our national life remains the imbalance in the way we are all educated. Resources are deliberately skewed towards the needs of those who already have access to culture. Unlike the French, or even the Scots, the English seem, as a people, incapable of exercising the willpower or imagination to invent an educational system in which cultural aspiration is seen to be the right of everyone, and not just a well-provided middle class. To quote a penetrating observation of Tawney's: 'Opportunities to rise are no substitute for a general diffusion of the means of civilisation.'

It is always with this essential caveat that you speak at all about the quality of work in any of the arts in my home country. Marxism may well have failed as a creed, but it still has its values as a method. Sometimes it may remind you of certain valuable truths: in this case that the quality and nature of the plays being written at any time will crucially depend on who in the society is empowered to write them. But even given that massive reservation in what I am arguing, it does trouble me that the younger generation of playwrights with which the British theatre is now richly blessed seem not able to work their way out of the studio theatres in which their work is largely developed and to find their way onto bigger stages where they might make some more general impact on the culture at large.

That this new generation exists at all may be seen to be a matter of wonder and surprise. When Stephen Daldry at the Royal Court, and Nicholas Wright at the National Theatre, tell us that for the first time in years they are receiving through the post fully-fledged plays from young writers whose names they do not recognise, and which are ready for, and deserving of, immediate production, then we may conclude that all the easy cultural theorising of the last ten years has turned out to a be a load of nonsense. Contrary to the propaganda of the period, young writers are indeed turning unexpectedly to the poor, beleaguered theatre – in particular to places like the Bush, the Traverse and the Theatre Upstairs – as venues which they think attractive and worthwhile. But at the same time, while welcoming their presence and wishing them whatever they need – either the courage or the fool-hardiness – to choose to make their whole lives in the theatre, I am disturbed by the fact that none of them has yet provided that kind of rallying point which every theatregoing generation needs to provide a focus for its own wishes and dreams.

The ability to hit your time is of course not the only thing that a playwright needs. Perhaps it is not finally even the most important. And it may one day be the reason why your work is superseded and forgotten. Who, in a hundred years' time, will read the most interesting work of our period without exhaustive footnotes? But surely we all sense that some essential fun, some special vigour goes out of the business of the theatre at large unless at any one time it displays some writers who have the special gift for seeming to make the form itself topical and urgent. In an unguarded moment I once said that *Look Back in Anger* was the modern play I would most like to have written. Since then hostile critics have quoted the remark to tar me with whatever brush they happen to have in their hand at the time. But what I really meant was that *Look Back in Anger* was the play whose effect I would most like to have provoked. Plainly, in our lifetime, it is unlikely that another play will have a comparable effect, although, on a smaller scale, Caryl Churchill has been heard with a similar passion by her audience, and Tony Kushner by his. But – and here is a point I would make 'with my hand in the fire' – to me it is true, true beyond anything, that if at least the *ambition* to be urgently contemporary goes out of our theatre, then we will have lost the thing which most distinguishes it and makes it valuable.

If, at this moment, you take my remarks for needless piety, merely the expression of views which are felt widely to be held in common, if you doubt that some essential determination is going out of the character of some of the people who lead our theatre, then please consider the fact that the Royal Shakespeare Company – the same Royal Shakespeare Company which endlessly reiterates our national playwright – has now altogether betrayed its intention to present new plays on its main stages. (The artistic director of the RSC did once write to me asking for a play. The fact that he sent his letter to an address I had vacated fifteen years previously gives you some picture of the dusty state of his Jacobean Rolodex.) When Peter Hall founded the company in 1960, then he fought hard for the principle that a true classical ensemble would need to be stretched and challenged by work from living writers. If the RSC was not to go the way of the Comédie Française, Pinter would have to enjoy equal status with the Elizabethans. Yet if any single trend has distinguished the last ten years, not just at the RSC, it has been the growth of an increasingly obtrusive directocracy, few of whom seem to feel much responsibility to the writers of their own period. Most of them have practised their flashier effects on the work of playwrights who were all too conveniently dead to protest.

The prosperity and vitality of the post-war period of

British theatre was marked out by a series of lively partnerships between directors and playwrights. Dexter worked with Shaffer, Blakemore with Nichols, Eyre with Griffiths, Gaskill with Bond, Stafford-Clark with Churchill. At one time, every dramatist seemed to boast a regular director as loyal and companionable as a partner or husband – it was, if you like, *Seven Brides for Seven Brothers* – but the results were excellent. In recent years, however, it has been noticeable that some directors have become frightened to work with partners of at least equal intellect and ability who are also inconveniently alive and present in the rehearsal room to engage them in fruitful dialogue about the direction of their own ideas.

This split, which is growing, between those who determine our dramatic repertory and those who still want to write about the lives we are now leading has benefited neither director nor writer. The work of many such directors is prematurely studied and dull, while writers, correspondingly, are encouraged to be unambitious. Up until recently in Britain we had happily escaped the wilder excesses of Director's Theatre with all its naff ideas and its opportunities for largely arbitrary pieces of self-advertisement. We liked to regard a play as something which worked in an intended area of meaning. Even if, clearly, a play could not be reduced simply to its author's conception – that would leave the astonishing creativity of British acting out of the equation – nevertheless a play was not just a toy with which a director might mess around at will in order to advertise for further employment. Recently in France, after watching a play of mine end with a scene I had never written in which two elderly people waltzed to an accordion, while a procession of masked figures holding black umbrellas walked by in a shower of stage rain, through which you could dimly see a shadowy figure whom I managed to identify as Elizabeth II, I politely asked the director what all this had to do with a play whose ostensible subject I had always taken to be the British Labour Party. 'Ah,' he replied, 'that is what in France we call *le concepte*. What do you call that in English?' I answered: 'We have no such word in English.' If only it were true! Lately, as Arthur Miller has said, plays have been directed not for what they are, but for what they remind the director of. It was said, in a famous statement of the Royal Court ideal, that one should direct new plays as if they were classics, and classics as if they were new plays. Today too many classics are presented as if they need gussying up, and too many new plays are not presented at all.

It is hardly coincidence that this period of increasing directorial licence has occurred at the exact moment that our one-time leading classical company, the RSC, has plunged into apparently terminal crisis. As Peter Ansorge points out in his book *From Liverpool to Los Angeles*, there was a great furore in 1962 when Peter Brook chose to cut just two lines ('Go thou. I'll fetch some flax and whites of eggs / To apply to his bleeding face. Now heaven help him') from his justly admired production of *King Lear*. He was attacked for altering the whole balance of the play. But now the work of many of the newer classicists is so ingrown and so self-referential that whole swathes of text get butchered without anyone even caring very much. It is as if the British theatre is indeed now finally going the way of the French, dividing itself into three separate compartments – the classical, the boulevard, and the avant-garde – and thereby missing the rich exchange between the three, the area in the middle, out of which, in this century, has come most of our own most remarkable native work.

It is hard to understand why anyone would choose to go into the theatre in the first place unless they were interested in relating what they make happen on a stage to what is happening off it. Academicism in the theatre, of which we have an increasing amount, seems to me a far greater threat to its survival than commercialism. (Commercialism at least is in some sort of crude contact with its audience; academicism speaks only to itself.) I have long since given up hope of tracing the source of one of my favourite quotations, but there is scarcely a writing week when I do not think about it. Somewhere, somebody once said: 'All revolutions in art are a return to realism.' I do not think this remark referred to method or manner. It was intended to illuminate a danger to all art forms, which is to become cloistered, to turn inward. For this reason, the theatre perhaps, with its genuine comradeship and crackling gossip, drifts easily away from its moorings, and becomes unreal. Fresh life often appears when someone who is outside the form emerges from the street and shouts at the artistic community: 'No, you've got it wrong. *This* is what it's like.' Necessarily, those of us who have spent many years alone in a room with a fountain pen and a typewriter, cannot go on serving this function. The daily work pattern of being a writer is in itself isolating. It is tragic for us that Andrea Dunbar, one of these crucial writers best able to say, 'No, *this* is how it is,' died of a brain haemorrhage only a few years after she took up writing.

Obviously, if the climate of the time is as I have described it, I would have been inhuman if I had not sometimes begun to feel something of a dinosaur. I have worked so long in a form which is culturally ill-favoured, I have been told so often that the kind of social and political theatre which I love best is no longer of any interest to the theatregoer, that it would have needed far greater resources of confidence than those I possess not occasionally to feel that I, and some of the writers I admire most, are practising some sort of traditional folkcraft, which is being artificially sustained by people who have not realised how the world has changed. As I have watched dozens of young writers flare briefly, then dive off to California to drive coupés, or turn into blasé journalists practising the deadly trade of opinion, I have wondered whether more than twenty-five years' sustained engagement with the question of how to write a good play has really been a tremendously valuable way of spending my time on earth. In a hundred years' time, will my way of life be seen to have passed away completely? Yet at other times I have also been aware that, in some way which almost borders on an Oliver Stone-style conspiracy, this is precisely what the culture wants me to feel. At some primitive level, it profoundly annoys other people that our strange little sect still exists, believing in something which others think valueless, and willing to give up our whole lives towards seeking its perfection.

I was not lucky enough to know George Devine. By the time I arrived at the Royal Court, he had become a myth, and like all myths, somewhat irritating by the sheer variety of purposes to which he could be put by his different disciples. Yet in all their squabbling claims for the true direction of his example, there was one fact on which the disciples agreed and which even I, as a doubter, knew to be true: that Devine's struggle to insist, against the indifference of his time, that the new stage play had to be at the centre of the British theatre's work had literally cost him his life. He had died, they all said, of exhaustion.

Often it seems now that we are living through less urgent times. When the Cold War was at its height, then liberalising playwrights were attacked with open hostility. Now, in a less overtly ideological era, they seek to destroy us with neglect. I have no complaint about this for it may well do us good and, in the long run, it may even shrive our souls. The spotlight is not always the best place to work in. But what will be less forgivable is if the cause of the living playwright is abandoned by those who themselves work inside the theatre. Like everyone else, we live in uncertainty. We can never be sure that years ago we did not all board the wrong boat. But let the waves take us, not the crew's idleness.

The Play Is in the Air

This is the text of a talk given at a theatre conference at King's College, Cambridge, in 1978. It was my first lecture, a sustained attempt to formulate ideas which had been bothering me in a decade spent half on the fringe and half at the Royal Court and the National Theatre. Heckled on the day (including the unanswerable interjection 'Did Piscator die for this?'), and frequently challenged afterwards, it plunged me into a good deal of painful controversy. It addresses arguments underlying much of the dramatic turbulence described in Obedience, Struggle & Revolt.

To begin with the obvious: the playwright writes plays. He chooses plays as his way of speaking. If he could speak more clearly in a lecture, he would lecture; if polemic suited him, he'd be a journalist. But he chooses the theatre as the most subtle and complex way of addressing an audience he can find. Because of that, I used to turn down all invitations to speak in public, because I didn't want an audience to hear the tone of my voice. I don't like the idea that they can get a hand-down version of my plays sitting in a lecture hall and sizing me up. In the theatre I am saying complex and difficult things. I do not want them reduced either by my views on the world, or, more importantly, the audience's idea of my views. I want no preconceptions. I don't want, 'Oh, of course Hare is a well-known anti-vivisectionist, that's why there's that scene where the dog is disembowelled.' I want the dog cut up and the audience deciding for themselves if they like the sight or not.

The first lesson the playwright learns is that he is not going to be able to control an audience's reactions anyway; if he writes an eloquent play about the sufferings of the Jews in the Warsaw Ghetto there is always going to be someone in the audience who comes out completely satisfied with the evening, saying at last someone's had the guts to say it, those Nazis knew what they were about. As you can't control people's reactions to your plays, your duty is also not to reduce people's reactions, not to give them easy handles with which they can pigeonhole you, and come to comfortable terms with what you are saying.

So why, then, am I changing tack and beginning to try and speak a little in public about the theatre? It is partly because I have been trying in the last few months to put my ear to the ground and find out what a particular section of my audience is thinking and feeling; but it is also for other and very pressing reasons which I hope will become clear as I go on. I'd like to start with a story which has always taken my breath away, from Hardy's incomparable novel *Jude the Obscure*. The young mother, homeless in Oxford, living in appalling poverty with a family she cannot possibly support, puts her head in her hands, and says in the presence of her eldest boy, 'O, it is better if we had never been born.' Later that day she goes upstairs.

> At the back of the door were fixed two hooks for hanging garments, and from these the forms of [her] two youngest children were suspended, by a piece of box-cord round each of their necks, while from a nail a few yards off the body of little Jude was hanging in a similar manner. An overturned chair was near the eldest boy, and his glazed eyes were slanted into the room; but those of the girl and the baby were closed.

I always think this is the ultimate cautionary tale for playwrights. That someone will actually take you at your word. That you will whip yourself up into a fine frenzy of dramatic writing on stage, have your superbly played heroine step harrowingly to the front of the stage and cry out in despair, 'It is better that we had never been born,' and there will in fact be an answering shot from the back of the stalls and one of the customers will slump down dead having committed the sin of assuming that the playwright means what he says.

For this is an austere and demanding medium. It is a place where the playwright's ultimate sincerity and good faith is going to be tested and judged in a way that no other medium demands. As soon as a word is spoken on stage, it is tested. As soon as a line is put into the reconstruction of a particular event, it will be judged. In this way the theatre is the exact opposite art to journalism;

the bad journalist may throw off a series of casual and half-baked propositions, ill-considered, dashed-off, entertainment pieces to put forward a point of view which may or may not amuse, which may or may not be lasting, which may or may not be true; but were he once to hear those same words spoken out loud in a theatre he would begin to feel that terrible chill of being collectively judged and what had seemed light and trenchant and witty would suddenly seem flip and arch and silly.

Judgement. Judgement is at the heart of the theatre. A man steps forward and informs the audience of his intention to lifelong fidelity to his wife, while his hand, even as he speaks, drifts at random to the body of another woman. The most basic dramatic situation you can imagine; the gap between what he says and what we see him to be opens up, and in that gap we see something that makes theatre unique: that it exposes the difference between what a man says and what he does. That is why nothing on stage is so exciting as a great lie; why *Brassneck* never recovers as a play after its greatest liar is killed off at the end of the first act.

I would suggest crudely that one of the reasons for the theatre's possible authority, and for its recent general drift towards politics, is its unique suitability to illustrating an age in which men's ideals and men's practice bear no relation to each other; in which the public profession of, for example, socialism has often been reduced by the passage of history to wearying personal fetish, or even chronic personality disorder. The theatre is the best way of showing the gap between what is said and what is seen to be done, and that is why, ragged and gap-toothed as it is, it has still a far healthier potential than some of the other, poorer, abandoned arts.

To explain what I mean I should tell you of a conversation I once had with a famous satirist of the early sixties who has been pushed further and further into the margin of the culture, later and later into the reaches of the night on BBC2, or Radio Solent, or wherever they still finally let him practise his art. He said, 'I don't understand why every day I feel my own increasing irrelevance to the country I am meant to be satirising.' I suggested it is because satire depends upon ignorance. It is based on the proposition, 'If only you knew.' Thus the satirist can rail, 'If only you knew that Eden was on benzedrine throughout the Suez crisis, stoned out of his head and fancy-free; if only you knew that the crippled, stroke-raddled Churchill dribbled and farted in Cabinet for two years after a debilitating stroke, and nobody dared remove him; if only you knew that cabinet ministers sleep with tarts, that Tory MPs liaise with crooked architects and bent offshore bankers: if only you knew.' But finally. after his railing, the satirist may find that the audience replies, 'Well, we do know now; and we don't believe it will ever change. And knowing may well not affect what we think.'

This is the first stage of what I think Marxists call 'raising consciousness'; a worthy aim and yet. . . consciousness has been raised in this country for a good many years now and we seem further from radical political change than at any time in my life. The traditional function of the radical artist – 'Look at those Borgias; look at this bureaucracy' – has been undermined. We have looked. We have seen. We have known. And we have not changed. A pervasive cynicism paralyses public life. And the once-active, early-sixties satirist is left on the street corner, peddling pathetic grubby little scraps of sketch and song – Callaghan's love life? Roy Jenkins' taste for claret . . .

And so we must ask, against this background, what can the playwright accomplish that the satirist cannot? What tools does he have that the satirist lacks?

The first question a political playwright addresses himself to is: why is it that in advanced industrial societies the record of revolutionary activity is so very miserable, so very, very low? The urban proletariat in this country knows better than we ever can that they are selling their labour to capital; many of them know far better than we of the degradations of capitalism. Of the wretched and the inadequate housing into which many of them are born; of the grotesque, ever-worsening imbalance in the educational system whereby the chances of progress to examinability even at O level, even at CSE level, are still ludicrously low; of the functional and enslaving work they are going to have to do; of the lack of control they are going to suffer at their own workplace. Of all these things they know far more than we, and, most importantly, they are familiar with socialist ideas which see their sufferings as part of a soluble political pattern.

Worse, we have lived through a time of economic depression, which classically in Marxist theory is supposed to throw up those critical moments at which the proletariat may seize power. And yet, in my own estimate,

European countries have been more unstable during times of affluence than times of depression. It is hard to believe in the historical inevitability of something which has so frequently not happened, or rather, often been nearest to happening in places and circumstances furthest away from those predicted by the man who first suggested it.

Confronted by this apparent stasis, the English writer is inclined to answer with a stasis of his own: to sigh and imagine that the dialectic has completely packed in, or rather got stuck in some deep rift from which he cannot jump it out. And so he begins to lose faith in the possibility of movement at all. Compare this with a post-revolutionary society, like China, where the dialectic is actually seen to mean something in people's lives. In the play *Fanshen* it is dynamic. Political practice answers to theory and yet modifies it; the party answers to the people and is modified by it. The fight is for political structures which answer people's needs; and people themselves are changed by living out theoretical ideas. It is a story of change and progress.

Must it always be, however, that Marxist drama set in Europe reflects the state of revolutionary politics with an answering sluggishness of its own? By this, I mean that sinking of the heart when you go to a political play and find that the author really believes that certain questions have been answered even before the play has begun. Why do we so often have to endure the demeaning repetition of slogans which are seen not as transitional aids to understanding, but as ultimate solutions to men's problems? Why the insulting insistence in so much political theatre that a few gimcrack mottoes of the left will sort out the deep problems of reaction in modern England? Why the urge to caricature? Why the deadly stiffness of limb? Brecht uncoils the great sleeping length of his mind to give us, in everything but the greatest of his writing, exactly that impression, the god-like feeling that the questions have been answered before the play has begun. Even his idea of irony is insufferably coy. He parades it, he hangs it out to dry as if it were proof of the broadness of his mind. It should not need such demonstration.

I do understand the thinking. The Marxist playwright working in a fairly hostile medium feels that his first job is to declare his allegiance, to show his hand, if you like. He thinks that because the play itself is part of the class struggle, he must first say which side he is on and make that clear, before he proceeds to lay out the ideas of the play as fairly as he may. To me this approach is rubbish, it insults the audience's intelligence; more important, it insults their experience; most important, it is also a fundamental misunderstanding of what a play is. A play is not actors, a play is not a text; a play is what happens between the stage and the audience. A play is a performance. So if a play is to be a weapon in the class struggle, then that weapon is not going to be the things you are saying; it is the interaction of what you are saying and what the audience is thinking. The play is in the air. The woman in the balcony who yelled out during the famous performance of *Othello*, 'Can't you see what he's going to do, you stupid black fool?' expressed the life of that play better than any writer I ever knew; and understood

the nature of performance better than the slaves of
Marxist fashion.

I think this fact – that we are dealing, all of us, actors,
writers, directors, with something we cannot calibrate
because it is in the air and nowhere else – accounts for the
fact that theatre is often bound up in mysticism and why
it is known throughout the Western world as a palace
of boredom. Is there any boredom like boredom in the
theatre? Is there anything as grey, as soul-rotting, as
nerve-tearing, as being bored in the theatre, or as facing
the bleak statistical likelihood that you will be bored in
the theatre for ninety-nine per cent of the time you spend
there? I can sleep anywhere on earth, haystack, bus, railway station; I have slept soundly with mortar bombs land-
ing eight hundred yards away, yet I cannot sleep in the
theatre. This I put down to the fact that I cannot bear to
sleep when so many of my fellow human beings are in
such intolerable pain around me; not only my comrades
in the audience, but also my colleagues on stage. For if
theatre is judgement, it is also failure. It is failing, and failing, and failing.

I think that it is in some way to avoid this uncomfort-
able fact that dramatists have lately taken to brandishing
their political credentials as frequently as possible throughout their work, and that political theatre groups have
indulged in such appalling overkill: in some way to stave
off failure with an audience; to flaunt your sincerity, to
assert and reassert a simple scaffolding of belief in order
not to face the real and unpredictable dangers of a genuinely live performance is all a way of not being judged. It

is understandable, but it is wrong. It is in no way as craven as the scaffolding you will find in West End theatres, the repeated reassurances to the audience that narrow lives are the only lives worth leading; nor in my mind is it in any way as poisonous as the upper-middle-brow, intellectual comedies which have become the snob fashion of the day, meretricious structures full of bland references to ideas at which people laugh in order to prove that they have heard of them: the pianola of chic which tinkles night and day in Shaftesbury Avenue, and which is thought to be real music in the smart Sunday papers. The English theatre loves the joker, the detached observer, the man who stands outside; no wonder, faced with this ubiquity of tat, that political theatre tends to be strident and unthinking, not in its attitude to its content, but in its distrust of the essential nature of performance itself.

Historically it is hard for a serious playwright to be confident. History has not behaved in the way that was asked of it; and the medium itself in which we work has chronic doubts about its own audibility. Bronowski hectors from a corner of a tenement slum; while the Queen settles down on Fridays to watch *It Ain't Half Hot Mum*. The airways are saturated with conflicting messages. All a playwright can do is promise to speak only when he has something to say; but when he speaks, what special role can he assume?

For five years I have been writing history plays. I try to show the English their history. I write tribal pieces, trying to show how people behaved on this island, off this continental shelf, in this century. How this Empire vanished, how these ideals died. Reading Angus Calder's *The People's War* changed a lot of my thinking as a writer; an account of the Second World War through the eyes of ordinary people, it attempts a complete alternative history to the phoney and corrupting history I was taught at school. Howard Brenton and I attempted in *Brassneck* to write what I have no doubt Calder would still write far better than we, an imagined subsequent volume, *The People's Peace*, as seen, in our case, through the lives of the petty bourgeoisie: builders, solicitors, brewers, politicians, the masonic gang who carve up provincial England. It was my first step into the past. When I first wrote, I wrote in the present day, I believed in a purely contemporary drama; so as I headed backwards, I worried I was avoiding the real difficulties of the day. It took me time to realise that the reason was, if you write about now, just today and nothing else, then you seem to be confronting only stasis, but if you begin to describe the undulations of history, if you write plays that cover passages of time, then you begin to find a sense of movement, of social change, if you like; and the facile hopelessness that comes from confronting the day and only the day, the room and only the room, begins to disappear and in its place the writer can offer a record of movement and variance.

You will see what I am arguing. The Marxist writer spends a great deal of time rebuking societies for not behaving in the way that he expected them to; but also, furious because change is not taking the form he would like it to, he denigrates or ignores the real changes which have taken place in the last thirty years. A great empire falls apart, offering, as it collapses, a last great wash of wealth through this country, unearned, unpaid for, a shudder of plenty, which has dissolved so many of the rules which kept the game in order. While intellectuals grope wildly for an answer, any answer to the moral challenge of collectivism, the citizens have spent and spent, after the war in time of wealth, but recently in a time of encroaching impoverishment. We are living through a great, groaning, yawling festival of change – but because this is England it is not always seen on the streets. In my view it is seen in the extraordinary intensity of people's personal despair, and it is to that despair that as a historical writer I choose to address myself time and time again: in *Teeth 'n' Smiles*, in *Knuckle*, in *Plenty*.

I feel exactly as Tom Wolfe does in a marvellous account of his opportunities as a writer:

> About the time I came to New York . . . the most serious novelists abandoned the richest terrain of the novel: namely, society, the social tableau, manners and morals, the whole business of the 'way we live now'. There is no novelist who captures the sixties in America or even in New York in the same sense that Thackeray was the chronicler of London in the 1840s and Balzac was the chronicler of Paris and all of France . . . That was marvellous for journalists, I tell you that. The sixties were one of the most extraordinary decades in American history in terms of manners and morals. Manners and morals *were* history in the sixties. I couldn't

believe the scene I saw spread out before me. But what really amazed me as a writer I had it practically all to myself . . . As fast as I could possibly do it, I was turning out articles on this amazing spectacle I saw bubbling and screaming right there . . . and all the while I knew that some enterprising novelist was going to come along and do the whole marvellous scene in one gigantic bold stroke. It was so ready, so ripe – beckoning . . . and it never happened.

I can't tell you how accurately that expresses a feeling I have always had as a playwright and which I know colleagues have experienced, that sense that the greater part of the culture is simply looking at the wrong things. I became a writer by default, to fill in the gaps, to work on the areas of the fresco which were simply ignored, or appropriated for the shallowest purposes: rock music, black propaganda, gun-selling, diplomacy. And yet I cannot believe to this day that a more talented writer will not come along and *do* the whole scene. In common with other writers who look with their own eyes, I have been abused in the newspapers for being hysterical, strident and obscene, when all I was doing was observing the passing scene, its stridency, its hysteria, its obscenity; and trying to put it in a historical context which the literary community seems pathologically incapable of contemplating. In *Teeth 'n' Smiles* a girl chooses to go to prison because it will give her an experience of suffering which is bound in her eyes to be more worthwhile than the life she could lead outside: not one English critic could bring himself to mention this central event in the play, its plausibility, its implications. It was beyond their scope to engage with such an idea. And yet, how many people here have close friends who have taken control of their own lives, only to destroy them?

We are drawing close, I think, to what I hope a playwright can do. He can put people's sufferings in a historical context; and by doing that, he can help to explain their pain. But what I mean by history will not be the mechanised absolving force theorists would like it to be; it will be those strange uneasy factors that make a place here and nowhere else, make a time now and no other time. A theatre which is exclusively personal, just a place of private psychology, is inclined to self-indulgence; a theatre which is just social is inclined to unreality, to the impatient blindness I've talked about today. Yeats said, out of our quarrel with others, we make rhetoric, while out of our quarrel with ourselves, we make poetry. I value both, and value the theatre as a place where both are given weight.

I write love stories. Most of my plays are that. Over and over again I have written about romantic love, because it never goes away. And the view of the world it provides, the dislocation it offers, is the most intense experience that many people know on earth.

And I write comedy because. . . such ideas as the one I have just uttered make me laugh.

And I write about politics because the challenge of communism, in however debased and ugly a form, is to ask whether the criteria by which we have been brought up are right; whether what each of us experiences uniquely really is what makes us valuable; whether every man should really be his own cocktail; or whether our criteria could and should be collective, and if they were, whether we would be any happier. However absolute the sufferings of people in the totalitarian Soviet countries, however decadent the current life of the West, the fact is that this question has only just been asked, and we have not even the first hundredth of an answer. To give up now would be death.

I said at the beginning that I have chosen to speak, in part simply to find out, to put my ear to the ground. And I must tell you what I find in universities. I find a generation who are cowed, who seem to have given up on the possibility of change, who seem to think that most of the experiments you could make with the human spirit are likely to be doomed or at any rate highly embarrassing. There is a demeaning nostalgia for the radicalism of the late sixties, people wanting to know exactly what the Vietnam marches were like. To me it would be sad if a whole generation's lives were shaped by the fact that a belief in change had fallen temporarily out of fashion; in Tom Wolfe's terms, it would be sad if this historical period had no chronicler.

Our lives must be refreshed with images which are not official, not approved; that break what George Orwell called 'the Geneva Conventions of the mind'. These images may come on television, something of a poisoned well in my view, because of its preference for censoring its own best work, or simply banning it; or they may come in this unique arena of judgement, the theatre.

I find it strange to theorise. Mostly theatre is hard work and nothing else. It is no coincidence that some of the British theatre's loudest theorists are notoriously incompetent inside a rehearsal room. It is a different kind of work. The patterns that I've made today in my own work and talking about others are purely retrospective, just the afterbirth; the wonder of performance is – you will always be surprised. The short, angry, sandy-haired, squat playwright turns out to write plays which you experience as slow, languorous, relaxed and elegant: the great night you had in the theatre two years ago turns out upon rereading to be a piece of stinking fish. I would wish it no other way.

An old American vaudevillian of the thirties drank his career away, fell into universal disfavour, but was finally found and put into an old people's home in California by a kindly producer who had once worked with him many years before. Visiting the old actor on his deathbed, the producer said, 'You are facing death. Is it as people describe? Is there a final sense of reassurance, a feeling of resignation, that sense of letting go that writers tell us consoles the dying?' 'Not at all,' said the comic. 'On the contrary. Death is none of those things that I was promised. It is ugly and fierce and degrading and violent. It is hard,' he said, 'hard as playing comedy.' All I would add is, not as hard as writing it.

What Asian Babes? What Nazis?

In 2001 I was asked to address the dinner of a group called the Solus Society, essentially an executive dining club for some of the longest serving and most senior people in the media. The prosperous membership was drawn from advertising, from television, from the cinema and from the press.

Playwrights don't get out much. I did once accept to speak in Westminster Abbey. I pointed out to the Dean that I wasn't a Christian. 'Exactly,' he said with the endearing logic of the Church of England. 'That's why we want you to speak.'

It feels as if something of the same logic obtains tonight. What reason can there be for inviting someone from the theatre, of all places, to speak to a gathering of media honchos, except because the theatre is now barely part of the media at all? Making my living mostly from the stage, I feel in roughly the same power relationship to the dominant media as an antic lute-player on a deserted hillside, or a potter in a barn somewhere in the Orkneys.

Perhaps my qualification is that I once, with Howard Brenton, wrote a play called *Pravda* about a mad South

African newspaper owner played by Anthony Hopkins as a kind of maquette for his subsequent Hannibal Lecter. Anxious lest our fictional proprietor be confused with a conspicuous real-life Australian, the Board of the nervous National Theatre insisted that we consult a QC. 'Well,' said this highly intelligent man, 'as far as I can see, your play portrays a megalomaniac psychopath who drags his newspapers downmarket, who has no concern for editorial standards, who has no sexual pleasure except in the public humiliation and violent dismissal of his staff, and whose only real interest is in the accumulation of a massive, unscrupulous and anti-social fortune for himself. If Rupert Murdoch really wants to step forward and identify himself as the hero of the play, then my advice would be: let him.'

In fact, Murdoch's response to the play was characteristic. In *Pravda*, our Lambert le Roux adopts British citizenship specifically in order to be able to own British newspapers. Please note, six months *after* our opening night Murdoch decided to become an American, protesting that, like Lambert, he went through 'the normal channels, albeit at unusual speed'. Murdoch effectively treated our play not as a work of art, but as an inspirational business plan. Is Murdoch the only man on earth who could actually asset-strip a satire?

I think you could say that Fleet Street was divided in response to *Pravda*. Tribute was paid to us in the newsroom of the *Daily Mail* where reporters shouted for a while in thick Afrikaner accents. But there was another faction who regarded the whole thing as an outrageous libel on their dignity and honour. What right did two people who had never been journalists have to abuse the high principles of their calling? What were our qualifications? What special insight or knowledge did we have? What research had we done? As commentators flung themselves into that kind of hysterical self-righteousness which affects the British journalist only when discussing his own profession – everyone else, of course, is just there to be pissed on – my friend Howard Brenton made a magisterial reply and one whose relevance I want to press on you tonight. What research had we done? *We had read the papers.*

Yes, that's it. For six weeks we took every national and some regionals, and read them from cover to cover. If you think this is not unusual, then let me tell you of a conversation I had the other day with the editor of a leading broadsheet title. I asked him this very question. Had he ever read an entire issue of his own paper? 'Don't be ridiculous,' he said. ' Have you ever seen an issue of my paper? Do you know how thick it is?' I asked him, 'Have you ever read that section about education?' 'Well, I've seen it, I can't say I've ever read it.' 'Or the one about social trends?' 'Of course not.' 'Motoring?' 'Please.' The internet supplement? 'Hold on, are you pulling my leg . . .'

So now you understand who I am, and maybe even what I think I'm doing here. I have a special area of expertise, one not shared by everybody in this room. I am the poor sod who actually reads your papers and watches your television programmes and buys your books and considers your advertisements because, unlike nearly everybody else at this dinner, I am one of the few people who has time to. I do not, like executives at the BBC, go to my weekend cottage with a cartload of tapes which I dispatch on fast-forward. Nor am I whisked round town in a chauffeur-driven car scanning only the front and news pages of rival publications. On the contrary. I am the nearest here to a dispassionate consumer of your raw material, of the logorrhoeac flood of video and print under which the country groans. Anyone who has watched the elephants at London Zoo fanning with their tails through each other's deposits for any scrap of remaining nourishment will recognise me. I am the man, whisking my tail, who turns on the telly, and who picks up the paper in the hope of finding something good.

How, you may ask, am I doing?

I said just now I was dispassionate but I admit one piece of personal bias. Television lost most of its appeal for me as a viewer when it abandoned the single play. It was once agreed that British television would not be able to compete with the American genius for group-authored series, with teams of writers working to producer-invented storylines. Instead British television would play to its own local strength. It is not in the slightest nostalgia which has me regretting a genre which produced Dennis Potter, Ken Loach and Troy Kennedy Martin, writing sixty- and ninety-minute films which attracted eight or nine million viewers at peak times. Rather the opposite. It is a much more hard-headed consideration. Single drama is what we were good at. Imitating American drama is what we're hopeless at.

And yet in a spirit of wilful jealousy the controllers at the BBC murdered the only genre – apart from its natural history programmes – for which the organisation was admired worldwide.

I once had an interesting conversation with the excellent John Thaw, who told me that his life had been much more difficult since an order went out from the Head Scheduler at ITV saying that they would do any drama, didn't matter what, as long as it starred David Jason, John Thaw or Robson Green. This had meant, John said, that a ridiculous number of scripts were being submitted to him by speculative producers who knew that John's acceptance would mean an automatic goer. 'The point is, you see,' John went on, 'along with Robson Green and David Jason, I am now effectively controller of drama at ITV. And that is not a post we ever applied for.'

It is too much to ask that anyone within British television should be ashamed of its current priorities. Those of us who work in the theatre and who endure countless newspaper articles on 'The Death of the Theatre' have noticed that representatives of the mightier media do not seem to discuss their own decline or imminent demise with quite the same relish they bring to predicting everybody else's. Indeed, although both newspaper readership and television viewing are demonstrably falling far faster than theatre attendances, you might even observe that they do not discuss it at all. Self-criticism is not the strong media's strong point. Multi-channel choice, with all its inflationary over-production, is, perversely, not giving freedom to the individual writer, who you might think would be left to get on with things unhindered, but rather imposes ever-more laboursome and fatuous layers of management (as we call it in the private sector) or bureaucracy (as we call it in the public). Nothing in television now moves with the speed of a good idea.

I know one veteran American director who told me that he is old enough to have worked in Hollywood before the concept of 'input' was invented. If, like me at the moment, you are writing for an American studio – very happily, I must add – then you understand that you are making an implicit deal. Because they are financing the film, they are effectively buying the right at any time of day or night to wake you with their insights into how the film might be improved; they have the further right, both in filming and editing, to disregard and violate every word and image you have written, and replace them with words and images of their own; and finally, if they so choose, they may remove the lungs, liver and heart from your precious dream, flambé them in brandy and cream and serve them with the popcorn they flog in the lobby. In return for that right, you are fabulously well paid. British television has copied from America all the techniques of interference, input and travesty, without remembering that last essential detail: that the writer is meant to get paid for it as well.

You may argue that in the theatre we take self-doubt to ridiculous lengths. Richard Eyre recently delighted his enemies by denouncing the medium in which he has made his living, including his own outstanding tenure at the National Theatre, with a flagellating fervour which reminded me almost of Chris Woodhead – a man whose qualification for leading the teaching profession appears to be a deep hatred of teachers. (Tony Blair, the leader of the Labour Party, is similarly afflicted by more than a passing distrust of socialists.) But I cannot see how any serious television executive, however plumply commercial, is not now sitting at his or her desk asking him or herself why British television no longer produces the excitement of *The West Wing* or *The Sopranos*. We have bought into the corporate, ratings-obsessed thinking of the US, while forgetting that this density of drama needs lavish investment of capital. As so often, and in so much, we feebly imitate America's competitiveness, while ignoring its balancing generosity.

I want, further, to suggest that the problem has a second reason, which is at the heart of what I'm saying tonight. In the days when every moment of output did not have to be supervised to destruction, television departments worked on the things they were best at. Before television refined its present autocratic procedures, with distracted and over-busy channel controllers having individually to approve each choice made on behalf of an art-form for which they have no feeling and to which, conspicuously, they believe themselves too important to give much time, then qualified Heads of Drama – most of them, by the way, trained in the theatre – worked in forms they profoundly understood. They did not have to wait days, weeks, months, even years, as they now do, for the simplest decision from people whose staggering rudeness towards creative personnel makes them incapable of speedily reading a script. In those days of comparative autonomy, it did not matter – except in egregious cases of censorship – that people from current affairs were always promoted over people from the arts to take positions of power in television. But now that producers and writers are no longer trusted to get on with their own work, that same preferment matters enormously. TV is run by journalists. And many journalists temperamentally do not understand drama.

Journalistic culture is everywhere in the ascendant. Watching *The Late Review* the other night, I listened patiently while the four journalists in the studio condemned everything that came before them with what John Osborne called 'the yawn and spite of fashion'. The movie under consideration was, unsurprisingly, judged to be a failure. The exhibition? Little better. The book? Beneath contempt. It was only when the programme paid tribute to the death of a fellow-journalist that at last something and somebody was found who could be approved. It seemed not to occur to any one of these four pedal-to-the-metal critics that the sum of their views might just be a tiny bit coloured by their own perspective.

John Diamond, I should make plain, was said, in report, to be a valiant, articulate man who remained witty and acute through terrible suffering. So, as it happens, did my friend Louis Malle, whose own last, cruel year was marked out by similar torment. Louis was a great film director whose work touched and moved as many people as Diamond's, often in ways to which Diamond himself would not have claimed to aspire. This is the man who made *Lift to the Scaffold*, *Les Amants*, *Souffle au Coeur*, *Au Revoir les Enfants*, *Lacombe Lucien*, *Atlantic City*, *My Dinner with André* and *Vanya on 42nd Street*. Let us say, to put it no higher, that there are probably fewer than twenty film-makers who ever lived who can boast an output of this distinction. Yet Louis' death was conspicuously not greeted with the same encomia that are extended by journalists to journalists. On the contrary, Malle's work, in the Chekhovian breadth and consistency of its humanity, seemed to represent some kind of personal assault on the glibber values of those assigned to mark his passing.

When I read in one newspaper that Auberon Waugh, an intermittently funny columnist, was in fact a far greater writer than his father Evelyn, whom I had hitherto assumed to be one of the century's most original novelists, then I did begin to feel that journalism has become an excessively silly, self-serving, backslapping cartel whose primary purpose is to damn anyone outside the gilded profession and to eulogise anyone within. Artists? Fakes. Actors? Bubble-heads. Politicians? Crooks. Social workers? Incompetents. Doctors? Organ-stealers. Asylum seekers? Liars, thieves and a threat to the British way of life. Journalists? Sadly, sadly undervalued.

The writer Richard Curtis told me that he stopped taking *The Independent* when a film journalist, in his obituary, pronounced the film director David Lean 'a semifascist'. I told Curtis it was an interesting coincidence because I myself had never paid money for that same paper since the day after Nureyev died, when its front page announced that the dancer was a vain and shallow man who had gone on dancing too long and who wasn't that good in the first place. (*The Independent*, let us remember, is the paper which was set up to be the alternative to Fleet Street, not its quintessence). The same writer who slandered Lean was also leader of the gang who were allowed by their nodding editors to lay into Louis Malle, secure in the knowledge that they themselves will one day step into their own graves, flashing passports marked 'Journalistic Immunity'.

I want to conclude these media-friendly remarks by reassuring everyone here that there is, thankfully, one certain means of reining in the arrogance of the new media class, who condemn everything but themselves. There is one person who has heroically proved that it may be possible for a lonely individual to have some recourse when he feels himself traduced by the press. I refer, of course, to the remarkable Richard Desmond. Branded a pornographer by the *Daily Mail*, Desmond retaliated by pointing out in his own *Daily Express* not only that the *Mail* enthusiastically supported Adolf Hitler, but, more poignantly, that the late Lord Rothermere's effervescent sexual history did not seem to square with his own publications' sanctimonious approach to questions of family morality.

The discovery that by subsequently meeting in a London hotel one newspaper group can do a deal to stop another newspaper group from printing what is, after all, the truth about each other, seems to me to take British publishing into a new area of corruption. In some corner of our souls, most of us know that the powerful care only about the powerful. But it is still startling to see it demonstrated with quite such overt public contempt. The executives of the *Mail* and the *Express* are effectively telling us that, as controllers of the media, they have the right to extend special exemptions from the savagery of the media *only* to each other. Not even Howard Brenton and I would have dared invent a scene in which a fouled and polluted news source agreed: 'I won't mention *Asian Babes*, if you don't mention the Nazis.' I think we may safely predict that the *Daily Mail* will not be meeting representatives of *The Asylum Seekers' Gazette* or of *Single Mothers' Weekly* to make similarly cosy arrangements.

At the end, let me be clear that, thankfully, there are traces of proper journalism remaining. You can read and draw comfort from a number of writers who still bother to report the passing show, rather than simply to advertise their own disdain for it. Because television has become almost entirely in its structures of power a journalistic medium, BBC journalism still has massive strengths of thoroughness and integrity. And there are occasional first-rate writers and producers making great television drama in a system which seems specifically designed to prevent it. When journalism fails, it fails for the same reason that art sometimes fails: because the writer lacked the imaginative ability to convey what it is like to be someone else.

This ambition of reaching beyond yourself by the exercise of your own imagination is undertaken daily on ignored canvases, in ignored theatres and by ignored poets all over Great Britain and Northern Ireland. It is only, by extension, the exercise of the faculty which makes us all human – the ability to project yourself out of the context of your own needs, sufferings and obsessions into the needs, sufferings, and obsessions of others. It is my impression that when as artists we fail, as we often do, it is because we have imagined insufficiently. But my impression of great swathes of modern journalism is that it is not even trying.

The Cordless Phone

In my lifetime, political theatre has been declared living or dead at regular intervals. Faced with such diagnoses, you always want to scream, 'Yes, of course it's uneven. It's an art form, for goodness' sake.' But in 2003 I was asked to contribute to a more considered series of articles by dramatists, mostly much younger, in the Guardian Saturday Review *which all addressed, in different ways, the general topic of politics in the theatre.*

The formative, founding lesson I had in political theatre came from the Artistic Director, William Gaskill, who was my first boss at the Royal Court Theatre in 1969. Bill returned to report back to us all on an ambitious 'state of England' play which he had a seen at a well-known address. He was not impressed. Bill took, I remember, special exception to the fact that in order to make a telephone call, clumsily essential to the plot, the hero had been forced to bring on a small table bearing only a handset, and to plonk it down in the middle of a large, empty stage. The phone rang and the hero lifted it. By its side, uselessly, dangled a wire which plainly led nowhere. 'That,' said Bill, 'is not what I call political theatre.'

It would be fair to say that even before that moment of revelation I had some growing sense that there might be such a thing as a playwright who wished not simply to write plays, but also to try and think through all the implications of a theatre event. Like many people of my background, I had chosen drama in the hope of using it to advance political ends. I was, biologically, a parasite. As we careered along the British motorways, going from school to prison to university to army camp, presenting short, sharp, nasty illustrations of what we believed to be the endemic crisis in Western capitalism, none of us doubted that we had stumbled on an aesthetic which somehow matched the aggression of what we had to say. Our approach was deliberately brutal, artless, direct. But I could already see that once a playwright decided to forsake impromptu canteens and naked floors to shelter instead inside built-for-purpose playhouses – in order to write on a larger scale and for larger companies – then he or she would quickly be brought up short by more desperate challenges. How, within the presentation of a single play, can you refine the resources and context of a performance so that it best conveys what you had in mind by wanting to write the play in the first place?

You might argue that Gaskill's contempt for the ineptness of the previous evening was nothing more than a proper respect for professional craft. 'Style,' said Evelyn Waugh, 'is not just avoiding the cliché. It's avoiding the place where you can feel the cliché being avoided.' Theatre is often the most naff of all the arts. Getting the furniture on and off in a way which doesn't look stupid is, in theory, as important to the most floss-headed farce as it is to a work with pretensions. But Gaskill's point was, I think, more profound and searching than that. Nobody, he was arguing, could call themselves serious about what they wanted to say through the medium of theatre unless they were also alive to, and actively solving, the practical problems that particular medium presents. You cannot just slap things down. Bill had had the good fortune of having formed his ideas during a period whose most radical and influential figures – Joan Littlewood and Bertolt Brecht – had not wanted simply to put on plays. They had sought out whole new languages in which staging was at least as eloquent as dialogue, and in which every constituent element of an evening might be reconceived.

Some of these thoughts came back to me a few weeks ago in Birmingham when I went to see the Repertory Company's astonishing productions of *Racing Demon, Murmuring Judges* and *The Absence of War*. It was my intention, ten years ago, when writing these three plays for the National Theatre, to create a vast nine-hour canvas on which the audience might consider some of the problems facing people working in the law, the church and the Labour Party. More important, they might decide whether metaphors suggested by these subjects had any resonance with the experience of their own lives. It was nice, of course, if anyone chose to see the plays individually. But the point of the enterprise was to put them together. The whole was far, far more than the parts. So it was hard for me, as I looked round at the eight hundred other hardy souls on a blinding April day, to accept that I had fashioned a work, supposedly full of political urgency – in my mind at least – but which could only be staged in a massive act of institutional resolve after thirteen weeks' rehearsals and with a company of twenty-five.

In all theatre, there is some basic disproportion between the amount of effort which needs to go in, and the risk that so few people may take so little out. For those of us who respond to vulnerability, that's one of the things that makes theatre so moving. But in this case the disproportion was almost absurd. In future, when people said to me they had seen my work, I would be forced to answer 'No, you haven't.' Or rather, 'You haven't seen it remotely as I intend it, unless you happened to sit all day on one of two Saturdays in Birmingham earlier this year – or on one of just six autumnal Saturdays on the South Bank in London in 1993.'

Was it crazy, then, to have spent five years creating a sort of wrapped sculpture which will, in all likelihood, not be displayed again in anything like its entirety for yet another decade – if ever? And was it crazy to put so much endeavour into something which has, necessarily, been seen by no more than a few thousand people? I can only tell you, as I walked away from the Rep, it didn't *feel* crazy. I was sad, but not regretful. After all, those of us who have spent our lives on the British left have been saturated, soused, drowned in failure. Failure's our element. Theatre has changed as little as society. Yet many of us have ended up curiously buoyant, not, let's hope, consoled but rather braced by the beauty of what we're attempting, in art as much as in politics. We are sustained by the thing itself, its superb difficulty.

Even now, thirty years later, when it's clear that much of the free theatre we once loved has become sclerotic, choked up by damp-palmed development officers and fetid sponsorship deals, and patrolled from the watch-towers by a bureaucratic Arts Council which has sought to rob the activity of its very point – its spontaneity – it is remarkable how many of us feel that even if it has been a lifetime of failure, it has not been a lifetime of waste. Nobody needs to point out to us that much of what happens on the stage is, in the Gaskill sense, still *unconsidered*. Most evenings embody unthinking stage conventions, and do very little to suit the music to the instrument. But only we, and the odd lucky audience, know the joy of those few, opposite occasions when contemporary theatre comes good. Ambition of form matches ambition of content.

One day, sitting by chance at a cricket match next to Barry Norman, I listened to his impassioned hymn of praise for an energetic British period film which, clearly, he had loved to distraction. 'Yes,' I asked, 'but finally what's the picture saying?' The one-time presenter of *Film Night* looked at me as if I were mad, replying that this was not a question which was likely to matter much to the filmgoing audience. What's more, he said, it was probably a rule that the greater the film, the more irrelevant the question became. 'What's *Casablanca* about? What's *Citizen Kane* about?' I replied, on the contrary, it was blindingly clear what those two films were about, and if he really wanted to know, I would be all too happy to tell him – at length. Norman just smiled, as if I were a fool. But, if I'm honest, it bewilders me to this day how rarely this particular question is asked (it seems less and less). I thought then it was the most important question you could ask of any work of art. 'Finally, what's it saying?' And I still do.

Raymond Williams:
'I Can't Be a Father to Everyone'

In 1989 a request came from the Hay-on-Wye Festival to give a lecture in the name of my old university tutor. The Raymond Williams Lecture has, before and since, attracted an extraordinarily interesting and diverse group of speakers, including the present Archbishop of Canterbury – a tribute, you may say, to the power of Raymond's memory, and to the complicated respect he still commands. Raymond's widow, Joy, was present.

You wouldn't recognise Cambridge from when I went to study there in 1965. Awash with money and computers, rebuilt to accommodate wine bars and Laura Ashley, it stands now, its lawns trim, as tidy as Toytown, wholly transformed from the seedy, neglected place I knew in what people of my age must now accept were the last of the post-war years.

I was an asthmatic, so for me Cambridge, with its chilling mists and slate-grey skies, was the worst possible place to finish my formal education. After leaving school I had filled in the six available months before university by flying Icelandic Air – stopover, Reykjavik – to California, where there still existed an exotic Pacific culture of mellow, sweet surfboards and girls who cut their jeans off round their thighs. The result was that I arrived at university in a thoroughly bad temper from which I never quite managed to recover. Convinced that I was doing the wrong thing, I forsook memories of the campus at Santa Barbara, which gave straight on to the beach, to come instead, weak-chested, to study in a converted nunnery, built of flint, with Britain's leading Marxist, Raymond Williams.

In a later essay 'You're a Marxist, Aren't You?', Raymond makes great sport with how indiscriminately people now use that word. And of course he is right. It has become a genteel sort of insult. On certain lips 'Marxist' is used to cover for the much blunter 'communist', just as the squeamish say 'passing on' when they mean 'dying'. God knows, when at sixteen I had conceived the idea that I must now study with a Marxist, I had little idea of what such a person might be like. Temperamentally distrustful of establishments, I knew only that I must find someone who could teach me to make sense of my politics in my daily life.

I cannot say that my first sight of Raymond fulfilled my expectations. Here was an apparently genial man, who had for some reason adopted a manner older than his years. Looking at the biography in the front of one of his books, I realise now that he was only forty-three when I first met him, yet stories were already told of his once choosing to give a supervision with his naked feet in a mustard bath. His status and authority had prematurely aged him. His hair was swept back from his brow, his teeth were prominent, and he had a mild, lilting manner of speech. On the first day of our arrival he was telling us that we should probably not expect to see him again for another year. He was farming us out, as was his right, to his juniors, most of whom lived in terraced houses on the outskirts of town. We would walk or bicycle to our new supervisors, in our tweed jackets, smoking our pipes, our wretched views on Wordsworth or the Metaphysicals tucked under our arms, all the time complaining bitterly of how we had been abandoned.

I had only chosen Jesus College because Raymond was there. I was scarcely drawn to it by its other distinctions, which were two: a reputation for rowing, and for the existence of a prestigious club in which undergraduates and elderly dons pretended to be roosters together, clucking, making jokes about feathers and eggs, exhausting every available play they could on the word 'cock'. I could not have been more unsuited to the character of the college. Nor, I would have thought, could Raymond. Yet here he was, with his Marxist colleague Moses Finley, the distinguished ancient historian, two ferociously intelligent men, perched, conspicuous anomalies, non-oarsmen, non-hen-impersonators, using the college for nothing else but to teach. Or, in our case, not teach.

I was not entirely at ease with the study of English literature, and this was not wholly down to Raymond's reluctance to teach us. It was more particularly due to an aversion to the drawing up of lists. The study of literature at Cambridge was organised round the idea that our function was to give dignified approval to a collection of writers who were in some mysterious way held to be 'moral': George Eliot, D. H. Lawrence, Dickens, Jane Austen, William Blake. Approval was conversely to be withheld from another bunch who, if not exactly immoral, were nevertheless not positively 'moral' in the elusive Cambridge meaning of that word: Milton, Robert Graves, Evelyn Waugh, Thackeray, Trollope, Dryden, Sterne, W. H. Auden, Oscar Wilde . . . Oh yes, I hardly need say that the unapproved list turned out to be longer, and prosecuted with a vigour which was entirely missing in the defence of the approved. Wherein this 'moral' quality in literature lay I was never able to discover, though it was bound up in something called 'seriousness', which seemed to be equally hard to define. The purpose of litera-ture appeared to be to please critics. Writers should work to guidelines which must be in essence 'life-affirmative'. Yet in the Cambridge critics' own writing, there often seemed to be a meanness of spirit, which hardly affirmed life at all. I felt I had picked up most of what I needed to know about academia when I learnt how a particular don, Q. D. Leavis, had greeted her new Professor of English, L. C. Knights, in a Cambridge street: 'I would wish you in hell, but having met your wife I know you already live there.' 'Moral' to the marrow, eh?

Somewhere in the middle of my second year, I reached a turning point in my education. I was being instructed in aesthetics by a don from another college, who came out and said bluntly what I had long suspected. He informed me, as an absolute law, that profound feeling could only be stirred in people by first-rate works of art. Only by coming to understand what was the very best, and then coming to value it above all things, could readers experience the deepest satisfactions of art. I asked him where this left people who enjoyed a profound religious experience when contemplating the work of an artist whom superior people held to be bad. I gave Salvador Dali as an example. The don's scorn was complete. 'Anyone who when looking at a painting by Salvador Dali imagines himself to be experiencing anything is quite simply wrong.' *Wrong?* 'They are fooling themselves. They may think they are having an experience, but they are not.' *They are not?* 'Only worthwhile works of art can produce worthwhile emotions.' But, I said, pressing a little further, who is the legislator for the worthwhile? Who is to define 'worthwhile'? He looked at me as if the question answered itself. 'Well, me. And people like me,' he said.

It would be fair to say from this point on I lost a good deal of relish for my studies. I had no desire to train to be a non-commissioned officer in the Arts Police, patrolling literature for capital offences such as 'failure of seriousness', or 'writing while under the influence of immorality'. The attitude of my don implied such a contempt for the ordinary feelings of people that the inevitable result of all this list-making would surely be more to remove me from life than to plunge me into it. Outside the university, a Labour government was once more selling its own supporters down the river, the Americans were snared in an insane war in Vietnam, middle-class youth throughout the world was bursting with indignation. What on earth could this *judging* be to do with anything?

I suppose this is how I came to think of the theatre as real. The critical and the creative came to seem to me diametrically opposed. If the purpose of criticism was indeed to inform people that they had no right to enjoy what they had hitherto been enjoying, then the purpose of writing a play or a novel was surely to greet them with something they might recognise and find they liked, almost in spite of themselves.

In this matter Raymond was an unusual professor, for in his own critical volume on tragedy he included in the back of the book a play about Stalin, which he had written himself. It was widely held to be unperformable – as far as I know, it's not been seen on a stage – and yet there was in the act of his including it a foolhardiness which at once made him personally attractive. It was hard to imagine any other don who was willing to forsake the safety of telling dead writers what was wrong with their work to risk making a fool of himself by writing his own play.

We would see Raymond across the quadrangle, books under his arm, a Dylan cap worn at an unlikely angle on his head, entirely in a world of his own, waving and running if one of us caught his eye, and we began to understand exactly why he had not wanted to waste another year dragging yet another generation of students through the novels of Thomas Hardy. He seemed implicitly to share Auden's view that by the time students reach college, they should be ready to teach themselves. And beyond that, clearly, he wanted to write.

Only in the third year did his students finally confront

him. He had become so agile at avoiding us that when we turned up at the beginning of term there were no plans even for the usual cursory meeting. Instead, we were instructed to report to an old colleague of his, this time actually outside the city limits. Our suggested tutor was chiefly known for his highly coloured campaigns against eroticism in literature. He spent much of his time counting four-letter words in novels, and consulting with Swedish psychotherapists who had theories about the long-term mental damage done to people who had become addicted to reading descriptions of the physical act. He had published a letter in the *Guardian* about the links between Hitlerism and nudity. He was widely held to be utterly cracked. It was typical of Raymond's mood at the time that he was more concerned to help out an old friend who was in need of a few quid from tutorials than he was to prepare us for the rigours of the tripos exam.

I have since been reminded that what followed was a strike. I'm not sure. Were things really that dramatic? I remember only an ultimatum. His third-year students told Raymond that they had been lured to the world's dampest university on false pretences. They had come for his personal tuition, and they were going to sit in his rooms until he consented to give it. I do remember his discomfort, which was profound. In the autumn of 1967, it was not an easy situation for the intellectual leader of the academic left to find himself in. It was downright embarrassing. In London new radical newspapers were being started. New political factions were forming in an atmosphere of wild optimism and vitality. The organised and disorganised left were taking to the streets. There was barely a new grouping that did not want Raymond's blessing and guidance. Yet on his own home ground his concentration was being disturbed by a small, self-righteous bunch of students who were demanding instruction in a subject in which they did not even any longer believe.

It was, I think, our scepticism about the study of literature which particularly infuriated him. To him it was self-evident that the professional study of literature was worthwhile and rewarding. He had no doubts, for his personal experience allowed him none. He had been a working-class boy from the borders of Wales. Literature and its study had been for him the way out of his environment but, much more important, it had also been the means by which he had understood his own feelings about that environment. Acutely sensitive to personal suffering, Raymond remained throughout his life fascinated by social history. I have no proof of this, but I believe that he was drawn to his favourite subjects – the industrial revolution, the movement of people between town and country – because of his passionate concern that people who might otherwise find themselves victims of history should be able instead to understand their own circumstances. And there was, self-evidently to him, no fuller way to understand than through imaginative literature. It had done the trick for him. As a young man, it had broadened and expanded him. In a Welsh grammar school, it had helped him to find meaning in his own upbringing. But now a generation of middle-class students was appearing at Cambridge whose attitude to literature, to the stuff itself, was a good deal more ambiguous.

It is easy now, looking back, to see myself only as a precocious young man who confused the study of literature with literature itself. I became so contemptuous of the list-makers, that I came to believe that the books they listed could be of little practical use or value in trying to understand the present day. Because the critics' lists seemed so irrelevant to anything I understood as urgent or worthwhile, so I became suspicious of the claims of art, and merely amused by the personalities of those who made a living from it. A similar distemper marked my politics. Britain was transparently in crisis. Its institutions were bankrupt. Its ruling class was anathema. Its traditions were a joke. A favourite game among undergraduates of my year was to spend long, restful evenings arguing about where a single campaign of aerial bombardment might be directed to best effect: on Buckingham Palace, on the Palace of Westminster, or on the mean square mile of the City of London. There was rarely in our discussions any time for all the finer points of socialist theory which made up Raymond's work and life. Only one bright, shining idea was misappropriated from Marxism and given universal assent: that from its own terminal contradictions, Western society would surely burst asunder in an orgy of violence and civil unrest. What would then happen nobody could say.

Nothing in Raymond's behaviour so attracted my scorn as his decision in the winter of 1967 to bury himself away in his room and set to work with a team of curly-headed academics who arrived from London in Citroens to edit a project entitled *The May Day Manifesto*. This work, to be published on 1 May 1968, was to set out a comprehensive programme of socialist change for the Britain of the 1970s. A yellowing copy of the eventual Penguin Special still sits on my shelves, a reminder of the days when, as a sort of Sergeant Pepper album of the organised left, it offered me and my despairing chums a fathomless source of satirical energy. As students, we took from Raymond the well-made point that an 'idea', so called, is not anything manufactured by an intelligentsia behind closed doors, but is more truly the expression of a widespread feeling which has arisen among many people at a particular time, and which then needs to be articulated. But if, as Raymond so often insisted, culture was in that way ordinary, then why did a manifesto of political ideas have to be set out in precisely that excruciating jargon which has alienated so many potential supporters from an interest in socialism?

The matter of Raymond's style remained a mystery to me for many years. Why, for heaven's sake, could he not be clear? Or rather, why did he choose to write in a manner which could only be understood by other highly educated people, or by those already versed in the modish junk terminology of left-wing politics? Here was a man who believed that ideas should belong to the whole population, whose own best work had sprung out of his time as an adult education tutor, yet who persisted in ploughing through the English language as through a field of dry bones, periodically using his favourite words, 'long' and 'complex', to justify the tortuousness and complication of his sentences. How could this highly sophisticated man not see that unless he laid his thoughts out clearly and simply in everyday language, he had no chance of reaching the very people whose interests he sought to advance?

But it was not simply to the style of this enterprise that his students objected. It was, as we believed, to its fatal lack of realism. We could not see the point of spending the winter months in putting together a detailed programme for change in Britain when it had not the slightest chance of being effected. Anyone who was brought up in the fifties had a very clear understanding that they were a member of one of the most deeply reactionary societies in Western Europe. The high-flown ideas of a group of Cambridge intellectuals had not the slightest chance of influencing the statute book, nor of forming the revolutionary programme of some putative army which, before advancing down Oxford Street to seize the Post Office Tower, would pause in its stride to consult a small red book about what it should be doing in its first weeks in control.

Politics, in our view, was about power. And power was about property. England, pre-eminently in the British Isles, then as now, was a vastly rich country, in which the ownership of land and buildings was grotesquely disproportionate. It was childish to imagine that the huge vested interests of property and money would surrender a penny of their wealth without the bloodiest of armed struggles; and it was also childish and immature not to foresee that the outcome of any such struggle would be chaotic and unruly. Even if – a massive if – you momentarily allowed the possibility of revolution in this most unlikely of settings, then you would, in looking at other revolutions, see only a record of theory being thrown away and burnt in a high-octane mix of happenstance and realpolitik.

Nothing prepares us for this, and nothing makes us sadder, than the moment when we realise that, in England, the fight is to the death.

If I suggest that I was able to articulate this in my relationship with Raymond, let alone sit and argue it with him, then I do wrong to his memory. For we were simply two different animals, who sniffed distrustfully round each other: he always drawn to the long view of things, patient, discriminating, qualifying every sentence with another sentence, pointing up historical parallels in every situation, set and determined in the sifting process which was his life's work; me, wanting to be tough and weeping for change.

The experience of the twenty years which have since gone by has done little to change my instinctive view of things, though I would hope it has deepened it. I am less impulsive. If you ask me for the reasons for the chronic problems of reaction in the British, then it is to the character of their intimate lives, their attitude to their children, their ways of giving and failing to give love, to their uncertainties and crises of spirit I would look, rather than rely on the much more materialistic outlook I had when I was young. But those same twenty years have also vindicated an impression I had then, that we were about to embark on a period of history in which British public life would be marked out by one thing: that, as a people, we cannot agree on anything.

I am trying to suggest that my character and Raymond's, ostensibly so different, were in fact shaped by our varying emotional responses to a common set of facts. For one thing also distinguishes those who seek change in Britain: an overwhelming sense of their own powerlessness.

Recently in Rome, looking at the Church of St Peter, I found next to the altar two statues, the masterpieces of Gugliemo della Porta, representing the figures of Justice and Prudence. In the original carving, Justice had been nude. But her figure was so astonishingly beautiful that in the nineteenth century priests used to gather and become aroused by her. So, predictably, the Pope had ordered her to be clothed. And now, one hundred years later, her true figure is still hidden from view, for fear that if Justice is seen naked, she will drive the people crazy. This perfect parable, as eloquent perhaps about the Roman Catholic Church as it is about the beauty of Justice, underlies the life of all those who share a belief that things are not ordered in our country as they might be: that privilege is still unequally distributed and above all, that British institutions show no wish to be sensitive to more than one section of the population.

Raymond's response to this powerlessness was to set himself upon a life's work of patient elucidation. In his commitment, he was quite extraordinarily stubborn. When in 1964, Harold Wilson was elected Prime Minister, Raymond had infuriated his excited students – I have this only at second hand – by warning them that, like all previous Labour administrations, this one would now proceed systematically to betray both the people who had voted for it and the principles to which it had claimed to adhere. The students had better prepare now, on the night of victory, for the coming years of disillusionment, and steady themselves for a longer and longer fight. As in subsequent years he was proved so spectacularly right, then the attitude of his students hardened not into one of gratitude for his prescience, but into heartfelt resentment of this wise old bird whose passion for the moment seemed always to be elaborately qualified by his exquisite sense of history. Where was the fun? And where was the anger? If, as he believed, democratically elected governments were always pulled to the centre by the power of capital and the suffocating influence of traditional institutions, then where could young men and women get their hope for the future? Not, surely, in a life spent behind high walls, in the chilly Fens, grading Herbert against Donne, and discussing defects of style in comparative English literature.

For, yes, after our protests, after our sit-in, after what others have called our strike, Raymond reluctantly agreed to teach us. It is the governing irony of this memoir that I can now barely recall a single thing he said to me during the supervisions we finally spent together. It brings back something of the flavour of the times to remember that we insisted on his personal tuition not because we genuinely wanted to listen, but, more typically, because it was our 'right'.

I cannot excuse myself for the time I wasted being angry with Raymond. I was too stupid to realise that he understood me better than I understood myself. Attending an undergraduate production of *Uncle Vanya*, I identified with Vanya's anger at his one-time professor, the insufferable Serebyakov, in whom the young Vanya has believed and by whom he feels himself betrayed. For years nothing disturbed the self-righteousness of my version. Yet the truth of the situation was more nearly that I was too exercised and confused to take whatever help Raymond might have offered me.

Only one remark of his do I remember. After a particularly incoherent dissertation from me on the works of D. H. Lawrence, there was a long and moody silence. Raymond sat for a while, staring at my week's work, then took his pipe from his mouth, shook his head, and said, 'Lawrence, poor bugger. Poor bloody bugger . . .' He then put my essay down without any further comment at all. This judgement from the most gifted social and literary critic of his time on the foremost novelist of a previous generation has always seemed to me to carry a singular, even a definitive authority.

Soon after tripos, I was off. While my friends were on the barricades in Paris, I was sitting in a hot exam room, not quite fulfilling the rich promise which the college had detected in me when it had given me a scholarship three years before. With Tony Bicât, who had passed a similar three years in the same college, spending a sizeable personal inheritance on good suits and becoming a jazz drummer,

I arrived in London to work at Jim Haynes' inspirational Arts Laboratory, where young men and women could put on the plays they liked, in the way they liked, in order to shock an audience who had seen it all. One night, trying not to disturb a couple who were making love on the floor of the single dressing room in which our actors were preparing to go on, Tony and I resolved to make some sense of our convictions by taking theatre out of the metropolis and to all sorts of places where it was not usually expected. Another night, soon after, the only person in the auditorium was a large, genial man who seemed unsurprised to find himself the only member of the audience. Taking advantage of the tradition that a company need not perform when it outnumbers the spectators – in this case by a ratio of five to one – we suggested that we go, audience and actors, to the local pub, where for the first time I was introduced to Howard Brenton.

Often in my life I have thought I was breaking violently with the past only to discover a continuity which was apparent to everyone but me. In setting up a new travelling group, Portable Theatre, I believed I was putting Cambridge behind me as decisively as I could. How then do I explain that the first plays we chose to present to bewildered audiences in church halls up and down the country were taken from the diaries of August Strindberg and Franz Kafka? Yes, there was a foreign tilt of which Cambridge moralists would not have approved, morality being the peculiar property of the British, but, even so, what reaction were we expecting with such neurotic and abstruse material?

Only with Howard's arrival did we begin to look towards our own times. Even he had trouble getting there. He had originally planned to write a history of evil 'from Judas Iscariot to the present day' – I drafted the publicity sheet, so the phrase rolls effortlessly off my tongue – and yet he found himself obscurely obsessed with the figure of the mass murderer, John Reginald Christie, whom he resolved, for the purpose of the drama, to bury every night under a mound of screwed-up newspaper in a pen of chicken wire. With this startling image – Christie, in a darkened theatre, rising from his grave, holding the length of piping he used to gas his victims – Portable Theatre found itself and was truly born.

I now see the company as an early attempt to sidestep the problems of aesthetics. To an extent the theatre will always be a magnet for hobbyists, people who are drawn like trainspotters or matchbox fans to compare different performances of *Hamlet*. They form, if you like, a core audience, who survive over the years. Their overriding interest is in the maintenance and improvement of their collections, and so they will direct their attention not so much at what is said, as at the skills which are being used to say it. As young men, neither Tony nor I had any wish to have our work seen as being part of the English theatre. We wanted the audience to concentrate not on whether we did or did not belong with other groups and movements, nor on how our production standards compared with others, but instead on the violent urgency of what we had to say.

Raymond himself approaches this problem in what I still take to be his greatest essay, 'Culture is Ordinary'.

He attacks the use of the word 'good' in a morally neut-
ral context. He points out that people say a 'good' job
has been done when they mean it has been professionally
carried out, regardless of what the job was, and what
ultimate effect it would have. In this sense Nazis might
produce a 'good' newspaper. Or military leaders might
sophisticate 'good' methods of torture. In Raymond's
view a thing cannot be good unless it has a morally good
aim. To those of us who worked for Portable Theatre
in the late sixties, a 'good' play could only be one which
shocked and disturbed an audience into realising that the
ice they were skating on was perilously thin. Any other
kind of play could only be a distraction. Perhaps you
may feel now that we were a little narrow-minded. Yet
even today, when my mood is less apocalyptic, try as I may,
I find myself indifferent to the bulk of English theatre, in
which the same old plays are aimlessly revived, and the
shelves of the London Library are combed for the obscurest
examples of seventeenth-century writing. Shakespeare and
his contemporaries did not sit around discussing whether
it was worth reviving *Gamma Gurton's Needle*, and
whether it worked in modern dress. They were arguing
about which of them should write the next play.

Our way of focusing the audience's attention on our
message rather than our means was to deny ourselves the
luxury of finesse by tumbling a group of actors out of a
van into an apparently unsuitable space with only the
crudest and most makeshift scenery. Most of the plays were
short, subversive and aggressive. Once, in Workington,
the audience were still seated, waiting for us to take a

curtain call, even as our van sped beyond the city limits and away down the motorway.

In the years to come, newspaper journalists would cotton on and start to write much windier analyses of the politics of decline. Antagonists went straight from calling us hysterical to calling us passé. By the time we had presented a series of these plays, all round the country, arts centres were beginning to spring up. The new audiences we had deliberately sought were beginning to find themselves plugged in to what came to be called a circuit. The bureaucratic nightmare of a centrally controlled Arts Council funding, with the attendant apparatus of boards, sponsorships and five-year plans, began to lock the performing arts in Britain into an intractable grid. And suddenly, when we were told that our costumes were better than the Freehold's but that our lighting wasn't as good as Pip Simmons', we realised that aesthetics, like the sea, covers everything, and will always have its revenge.

I lost touch with Raymond, and I cannot say I thought much about him. When I was writing with Trevor Griffiths, who frequently referred to him, I remember being astonished that anyone who worked in the theatre should think it worthwhile to maintain a dialogue with dons, even with one who was himself a creative writer. Theatre was doing. Academics were children, who worked in an unreal world of their own making. They were spared the minute agony of seeing their ideas fail in front of an audience. Unlike playwrights, for whom every night brings unwelcome scrutiny, they could live inside their own illusions, talking only to one another in their private language. I thought of them as not grown up. Besides, Cambridge was flirting with something called structuralism, which downplayed the individual's imagination, and insisted that the writer was only a pen. The hand, meanwhile, was controlled largely by the social and economic conditions of the time. This depressing philosophy was not one to cheer the heart of a playwright. It was indicative of the way academics were once more turning their faces to the wall. The other day, one of the wittiest and cleverest structuralists in England, an ex-pupil of Raymond's, told me the whole thing was over. 'Oh, great,' I said. 'Does that mean I'm back in charge of my own work?' He looked at me a moment. 'Mostly. But not entirely,' he said.

Meanwhile, civil violence not having broken out in the way I had predicted, I found myself making crab-like progress towards two of the central institutions of the culture, fascinated by the challenge of how to write plays which filled up the huge stages at the National Theatre, and delighted at the opportunity of reaching the huge public who still watch drama on the BBC. When I argued with another television playwright that the audience was not sitting there in one lumpen mass, passively receiving everything and unable to distinguish between the programmes and the advertisements, I was, in my insistence that the audience can and do discriminate, unknowingly parroting Raymond. It was so long since I had read him that I imagined my ideas were my own.

In 1983, fifteen years had gone by since I had last spoken to my former teacher. Out of the blue, I was invited to the Cotswolds, where Raymond was to give the key-note lecture at a forthcoming literary festival. I was asked if I would attend, and then without preparation join him on the platform to give my view of what he had just said. By the happiest of chances, we did not even meet before his talk, so I had no idea of what was to come.

He started hesitantly, drawing on a passage from *The Long Revolution* to detail the W. H. Smith bestseller list of 1848. Of the books listed, not a single one was re-membered, except for one by Jane Austen, who managed to come in at number eight. Taking the moral from this, Raymond drew attention to the extraordinary fertility of artistic activity in the world today, and to the breakdown of the old categories. Demographically the world had expanded beyond recognition, so there were more artists practising than at any time in history. Wonderful poems were being written in the West Indies; great novels were coming out of Nigeria; from India came great films; in Britain the theatre was lively as never before. In the face of all this activity, he said, the critic had great difficulty con-cealing his anger. So much going on! And all out of control! The critic's first instinct was to resent so much energy, for energy is the enemy of order, and order is the critic's job. No sooner had he or she written his piece on the death of the novel than the novel turned out to be bursting with life in Latin America. Moving quickly to come to terms with that, the critic now found himself wrong-footed by being told of something even more interesting going on in Czechoslovakia. Modern writing was unruly in its sheer abundance. Nobody could put a value on anything.

How then was a critic to react to this apparent chaos? Raymond smiled. By embracing it, he said. Let's not worry too much, let's just be grateful. Let's not succumb to the myth that there's no great writing any more. Every generation of critics asks you to believe that. They will always pretend that they knew which one was Jane Austen all along. But here it is, a matter of historical record, that Jane Austen once went unremarked, one among many, no more and no less popular than many of her fellow novelists. Let's not endlessly complain about what's not being done. Indeed, if we feel so strongly, then let's do it ourselves. Let's not peddle all that tired stuff about standards. Let time make judgements, as surely it will. Meanwhile, for goodness' sake, let's celebrate what we have.

I have never seen Raymond's lecture written down, so if my paraphrase is selective, you must forgive me. You may detect, for instance, that the tones of our two voices have become merged. But this only reflects an excitement I felt when I realised that after so much misunderstanding, he and I were, in the vaulted hall of the Cheltenham Literary Festival, for the first time in our lives, about to see eye-to-eye. But I do not misremember the conversation that followed over cups of tea, in green china. 'Yes,' he said, 'you were right. And I knew you were right, when you argued that the study of literature as it was then practised at Cambridge was a worthless activity. Underneath all that judicious grading of literature lay an actual hostility to literature itself. But,' he said, 'at that time I could not admit it. For to admit it was to allow my own irrelevance. Only since I've given up teaching have I been able to see those years for what they were.'

Laughing together, we both relished the symmetry. While he had been travelling in my direction, I had been travelling in his. 'My politics at that time were a joke,' I said. 'I was so incensed, so personally outraged with the discovery that the country's leaders had no clothes on, that I could not imagine that my outrage was not universally shared. I could not understand why you, as a socialist, seemed so sanguine, so ready to go on discoursing in your own little world. Aflame with indignation, I projected that indignation onto my fellow countrymen and assumed violence was inevitable. But I've learnt since, in the long years of Heath and Callaghan and Thatcher, that a country may despise its leader with one part of its brain, and obey him or her with the other. Although I still love the power of that impulse which saw us all out on the streets shouting our heads off, I have also begun to value at last the quieter and more profound discernment which your kind of work represents.'

In any work of fiction which climaxed with this touching scene, pupil and teacher reunited after fifteen years and each envying the other the choices they had made, the two characters would be used to represent different qualities. Most conveniently it would be said that Raymond represented careful reason, and that I represented ignorant feeling. Yet to paint it that way would be to do Raymond the gravest injustice.

An academic who can begin an essay on culture with his own childhood bus journeys from Hereford Cathedral into the Black Mountains is already set apart from most of his colleagues in his understanding of what is important. Underpinning everything Raymond wrote is a sense of possibility. Men and women cannot begin to fulfil the potential of their imaginations, unless they are allowed to influence and control their working lives. ('The permissive society?' I remember him asking. 'Oh yes? Who's doing the permitting?') A society cannot be healthy unless the thoughts and feelings of working people are given the same cultural status as those of a privileged middle class. The impulse which moves Raymond's work all the time is one of deep emotional generosity, a readiness to share in the pleasures he had enjoyed, and a delight in watching other people come to value them.

In his writing he mixed this with a passion for the absolute truth. Only when you grasp this can you understand the problems of his style, even if you cannot forgive them. Reading his books is often like finding the world's most exciting ideas somehow trapped under the ice. It was Tony Bicât who finally revealed to me that he too had been mystified by the manner of Raymond's writing, until he realised that its very cumbersomeness came from a horror of conventional thinking and an absolute determination to make a sentence mean exactly what it meant and nothing else. Raymond could be simple when he wanted to. But he rarely did.

It is the fashion now to denigrate the sixties. Trendy right-wing politicians, in hollow affectation, pretend to trace this country's ills to those days. They talk about the loosening of social bonds, and the decline of respect. In a favourite joke of Raymond's, a class which throws its own male children out of its homes, aged seven or thirteen, is in a poor position to lecture others on family values. As the period of office of the Thatcher government gets longer and longer, so the excuses for its failure must be traced further and further back in time. We are told that the deep-rooted problems of British life stem from the sixties. The word 'deep-rooted' is used to mean 'before we came to power'. Humourless themselves, the politicians cannot understand that a sense of the ridiculous is precisely what motivated most of what went on at that time. A lot of us do not need to be told, twenty years later, that our behaviour was ridiculous. Most of us knew it perfectly well at the time. That was part of the point. The reason no actor has ever given a successful or unembarrassing performance of a hippie is the same reason no one will ever play Groucho Marx or Jimmy Durante successfully: you cannot impersonate people whose whole gift is for satirising themselves. The clothes, the hair, the language are now spoken of as if the inventors of these customs did not know that a joke was in the air. Yet the absurdity, both in Europe and America, did have a certain purpose. Everyone was angry. But for a while they used their sense of humour to turn away despair.

I did not see Raymond again, yet when I read of his death I could not believe another five years had gone by. Our meeting seemed fresh, for the comfort it had given me lasted in a way that took no account of time. A struggle had been resolved. And now he had died.

In writing this memoir, I have suggested that this relationship between us had some special significance. I now have no way of knowing what it meant to Raymond, nor would I ever like to have asked. I was only one of the thousands of pupils who passed through Raymond's hands and, for reasons I have tried to make clear, not one with whom he was especially engaged. His last words to me were to complain of the ubiquity and neediness of his acolytes. 'I can't be a father to everyone,' he said.

Last December the college which had once threatened me with expulsion invited me to be guest of honour at the Annual Fellows' Dinner. In the Upper Hall, surrounded by the portraits of famous scholars and benefactors, I reminisced with a senior tutor, who told me our experience of Raymond refusing to teach us had been repeated many times in Raymond's later years. I asked if the college had done anything about it. 'No,' he said. 'We accepted that a college like this should be magnanimous enough to give him its protection without insisting he fulfil his official obligations. Besides,' he said, 'we didn't have his telephone number.'

It is good to come here today and talk as truthfully as I can about what passed between us, happily in front of his family and friends, and in the part of the world where he was brought up. Yet the occasion is, as ever, kissed with contradiction. For, after accepting to speak today in Hay-on-Wye in Raymond's memory, I discovered, by an irony he himself would have relished, that the lecture was to be given at a festival sponsored by the *Sunday Times*.

For some years now, this newspaper has gone to great pains, in its editorial columns, to inform what it calls the intelligentsia of the country that it is out of step with the – what is the word? – 'entrepreneurial' mood of the times, and that, by their insistence on values beyond the purely personal, artists and writers make themselves objects of contempt to the kind of people who are putting Britain back on her feet.

Well, for myself, I can only say these are fine times to be out of step with. Considering the ugliness and malice with which the newspaper has conducted its campaign, I wondered for a moment why the *Sunday Times*, with all its self-importance and power, had never actually succeeded in making me angry. And I realised it is a trick of my character only to be truly angry with those whom I hold in the highest regard. Hearing that this newspaper planned to sponsor a literary festival, my first thought was not to wonder at their hypocrisy, but instead to think, 'Well, that's good. They want to make amends.' And I was grateful. It is a fact. From certain people we are grateful for anything. From others, great men, great women, we expect everything. May it always be so.

Harold Pinter: Going on Seventy

At the Soho Theatre in London in 2000, at a celebration of Harold Pinter's seventieth birthday, a group of playwrights from different generations were able to discuss how and why they'd come to Pinter, and what he now meant to them. As an extra treat – for the author is a lively player of his own work – Harold then acted in a scene from The Dumb Waiter.

I first heard of Harold Pinter when I was at school. I think I'd read a play of his when I was about thirteen, but it never occurred to me he actually existed. Later, our Modern Languages master, Harry Guest, went up to London for the weekend and attended an intense, smoky party in what for me was still the mythical capital city, and found himself in deep conversation with the most admired young playwright of the day. Harry told us about it during our French lesson soon after. To all of us schoolboys, stuck away in the freezing cold of Sussex in the early 1960s, it seemed an impossibly glamorous encounter. You may imagine my astonishment when I found that this same Harold Pinter, who seemed so alluringly continental, actually lived just five miles away, in the unlikely seaside town of Worthing. I wrote to him, of course, drawing his attention to this remarkable coincidence – that, unbeknown to him, he lived so close to a snotty little schoolboy who liked his work.

In those days Pinter seemed to spend a good part of his time warding off zealous commentary on his output. Since most of that commentary came wrapped in the head-freezing jargon of the day – 'failure of communication', 'hidden menace' and so on – I think he was wise to keep his distance. I, meanwhile, had been allocated the job of writing an essay for the school literary society. As I remember, it was called 'Osborne and Pinter: Two Types of Realism'. Like most such critical intruders, I received no reply. Even at that early age, I could see that Pinter was an unusual figure. Now, almost forty years later, it is clear that British culture has been distorted by a false, contemporary division between literature and the performing arts. In France you find Marguerite Duras, Sartre and Camus all regarding the theatre as one of the necessary, even one of the defining places for a person of letters to do their work. In Ireland, you find Beckett and Yeats with the same idea. Perversely, it is only here in what Betjeman called 'dear old, bloody old England', where the tradition of theatre has always been strongest, that a purple vein of snobbery runs through the broadsheet book pages and through the attitudes of some poets and novelists themselves. It is only here, in a country still marked out by its gift for the performing arts, that literary folk seem threatened by the prospect of working in a form founded in the notion of collaboration.

From the very start, Pinter was inspiring because he was an obvious intellectual, and not ashamed to show it. He was a man who had read and absorbed European ideas and who wanted to explode them, with a terrifying bang, into English working-class settings. Up till then, poets who strayed into the English-speaking theatre often seemed pretentious (Lawrence Durrell) or dazzlingly incompetent (T. S. Eliot). But Pinter was a rare example of someone who was able to marry the intensity of his vision to a simple, practical mastery of his form. One of the many things Pinter has done for the culture of his day is to remind the literary world that you don't always find a poet between the covers of a book.

The work of most good writers is born out of contradiction. Snoo Wilson once wrote perceptively that John Osborne was a perfect Edwardian because he embodied the most notable archetypes of the period: he was both gentleman and cad. Harold Pinter, by contrast, belongs firmly to the mid-twentieth century, because in him you find expressed the great struggle of the period – between primitive rage on the one hand and liberal generosity on the other. Anyone who meets Harold quickly becomes charmed by his volatility, which has always seemed to me only a by-product of his openness. Because Harold does actually listen to what you say, there is a better-than-even chance that he will also react to it. This surprises some people. As an artist, Pinter has an alarming range. He can play great, big major chords made up only of anger, indignation and contempt. But, at the other end of the instrument, Pinter can also unbalance you by reaching humour, grace and intense personal warmth.

Attending a recent revival of *The Homecoming*, directed by Roger Michell, I was reminded not just of how bold Pinter himself used to be, but how uncompromising the whole theatre was forty years ago in its willingness to shock and disturb its audience. Even after so many years, the play still took the audience aback, not in any obvious four-letter way, but because it was so naked, so shameless in its portrayal of a knock-down sexual struggle within a family. Never for a moment was the audience allowed the get-out of doubting that something real and important was at stake. Much is always made of Pinter's style. But his many imitators now copy the style and don't notice the content. The impact of this exceptional evening depended on Pinter keeping his guard high, so that he never once offered the spectator the easy handhold of an 'attitude' with which they might be able to take some simplified view of the events on the stage.

It's this uncompromising approach to an audience, this willingness to say 'take it or leave it' (again, in my view, both generous and brutal) which is, I believe, Pinter's most distinctive and lasting contribution to the theatre. It does not surprise me at all that the author himself was thrilled when, after a performance of *Ashes to Ashes* in New York, a member of the audience was heard to remark, 'And he has the brass balls to call this a play?' Rarely can a playwright have combined so much nerve, so much gall, with so much evil pleasure in that gall.

Beyond that, it's the familiar mark of a first-rate writer that we all have our own favoured part of his or her work. Ibsenites dispute over whether to prefer the verse plays or the social plays. Fans of John Ford argue fiercely about whether his Westerns go up- or downhill as he gets older. Pinter sometimes seems as various as his admirers, but my own playwright is the one who gives you the three-course luncheon, the same man who wrote a trio of formidable, full-length plays in quick succession – *The Birthday Party*, *The Caretaker* and *The Homecoming* – while managing with his spare hand to develop two of the most perfect screenplays ever offered to the British cinema, for Joseph Losey's films of *The Servant* and *Accident*. Something majestic happens when a minimalist decides to go the whole distance.

The interpretation of living writers' work is an approximate business at best, and, in Pinter's case, you never seem to find the critical tea-trolley in the same place twice. I don't find Michael Billington's attempts to prove that Harold was always a political playwright any more convincing than the things which were written when people lumped him, even more crudely, into the Theatre of the Absurd. It's quite clear that Harold – like Patrick White, whom he resembles in his late intransigence – went through a period of antagonism to politics, both in theatre and in life, which was as profound, in its way, as his more recent, exemplary advocacy of some very important causes. A lot of people like to claim that, without Beckett, Pinter couldn't have existed. Again, I can't say I really know what this means. With his own highly original temperament and technique, it seems hard to believe that Pinter wouldn't have burst out at us in one way or another.

If, on the occasion of his seventieth birthday, we want to agree on anything, then we can agree on this: Pinter did what Auden said a poet should do. He cleaned the gutters of the English language, so that it ever afterwards flowed more easily and more cleanly. We can also say that over his work and over his person hovers a sort of leonine, predatory spirit which is all the more powerful for being held under in a rigid discipline of form, or in a black suit. Almost alone among British playwrights he has excelled as much when adapting others and when writing for the screen as he has when writing for the stage. The essence of his singular appeal is that you sit down to every play or film he writes in certain expectation of the unexpected. In sum, this tribute from one writer to another: you never know what the hell's coming next.

Alan Clarke: Banned for Life

I wrote once and spoke once about Alan Clarke, the visionary British director who died in 1990 at the age of fifty-five. Because Alan's work was primarily in television, it took a decade, and the advocacy of many good people, for him to be accepted as one of our leading directors of film. I remember walking down a side street in San Francisco some time after his death and coming unawares upon the retrospective that had always been denied him at home and in his own lifetime. Alan is now as internationally recognised as any British director save Powell and Hitchcock: Gus van Sant's Elephant *is only one of many tributes. The first piece that follows is an obituary, the second a speech for his memorial service.*

I

To call Alan Clarke's late struggle against cancer heroic would be to mislead, for that word suggests nothing of the wit and good humour with which he faced death. His dying was informed with exactly the same depth of character and vitality which marked out his work as one of the few really influential directors in television drama's short and uneven history.

I was lucky enough as a young man to have my first television play directed by him. Later, his then-girlfriend cursed me in the middle of the night as Alan lay awake, endlessly marking his script and wondering whether it might be possible to do the thing better. None of this obsessiveness showed in the morning for, as well as any director I have seen, he understood the balance between preparation and spontaneity. He worked all night in order to be open to all suggestions in the morning. Yet nobody who enjoyed this apparent openness in him, the generous ease with which he listened to anyone – actors, production staff, crew – could mistake the urgency of his governing conviction: that the lives of working-class people should be afforded on television the same depth and passion which is usually given to middle-class subjects.

There was in him, as in his work, a strange mix of romance and realism. In many of the distinguished plays he directed throughout the 1970s, like his riveting pro-duction of David Yallop's recreation of the Craig-Bentley case *To Encourage the Others,* he sought to drag tele-ision back to considering the reality of ordinary people's lives. Yet another side of him – the side which drew him to David Rudkin's *Penda's Fen* – was streaked with a romantic intensity which was almost mystical.

As a teenager, he travelled from Liverpool to the US with a few friends, all intending to get jobs as miners, but ended up instead fascinated by theatre, and working as a junior stage manager in Buffalo. When he returned to England to work in the BBC studios and then on film, he seemed drawn over and over to showing young people in brutal surroundings. More and more, he threw the camera behind them and in among them, getting it to speak for them. In David Leland's *Made in Britain* he sided with the educationally hopeless and in *Scum,* Roy Minton's unyielding account of life in a contemporary borstal, he presented the lives of the inmates with such visceral power that the BBC considered its only proper response was to ban it forthwith.

It was, of course, Alan's misfortune to make his best work at a time when the people who ran the BBC showed no interest in the views of those who created their programmes. But Alan was too clever and too strong to allow himself to become their emotional victim. Anger was in him; but not bitterness. Through the last decade he learned from the lessons of *Scum.* In *Elephant*, his entirely silent rendering of a series of sectarian murders, he threw out the script and found a characteristically personal way of trying to get everyone to look afresh at life as it is lived in Northern Ireland. In the genially dirty *Rita, Sue and Bob Too,* adapted from her stage play by Andrea Dunbar, he made one of the few British films which is entirely free of lameness and piety. And finally, in Al Hunter's *The Firm*, he made what I think is one of the few authentic television masterpieces, a portrait of nouveau-riche football hooliganism so snapping with life, especially in Gary Oldman's playing, that you watch hypnotised, both drawn to the violence and horrified by it, in a knife-edge performance which only Alan had the skill and moral certainty to bring off.

Television gets sillier. People think they know how to make money, yes, but worse, they want unconsciously to

conform to what we are used to seeing. Alan, one among
very few, kept his eyes open, seeing life with a sort of tragic
passion which drew him, towards his death, more to the
American sensibility than the British. Alive or dead, he
reminds the rest of us to keep looking.

11

Perhaps like some other people here I only got to know
Alan well when he allowed me to: in the last few months
before he died. Up till then, he had always been a little
hard to get hold of. From the start, there were practical
difficulties in getting together with Alan. When we were
working together in 1972, I remember suggesting we go
for a drink after rehearsals. He gave me a rather pitying
look, as if only a first-time playwright would not know
that he was the one director in British television who
worked under the handicap of a lifetime ban from the
BBC Club. I noticed then it was something of which he
was inordinately proud. When, years later, I mentioned
the name of someone who I thought had been similarly
honoured, he was immediately dismissive. 'No, no, temporary. Temporary, David. With me it's for life.'

Alan talked a lot about hating the English, and in the
last years of his life turned his heart and his mind much
more towards North America, where he hoped to find
the freedom and open-mindedness which had first drawn
him there as a young man from Merseyside. The very
word 'club' has always puzzled me next to the word
'BBC', and I remember even then thinking it must be a
very strange club which expelled its most gifted member.

Indeed, the club awoke and reasserted itself in the late 1970s, pointing out to him the inconspicuous clause in the rules which forbids any member to make a film which either too accurately or too realistically seeks to depict the lives of the people watching the television. Along the fault-line created by the BBC's decision to ban Alan's film *Scum* flowed all the lousy decisions and abject behaviour which left the BBC, ten years later, having to fight to justify its existence to government. But my chief memory of that extraordinary time is of Alan, after an interminable and massively unconvincing speech by the steeliest and most charmless of the BBC administrators being asked if would like to say anything in reply. 'Not much,' he said. 'I was just wondering if anyone'll give me a transmitter for Christmas.'

The most significant artists of any generation are often those who serve to remind their fellow-practitioners that a particular art form has unknowingly, through the very familiarity of its conventions, strayed a long way from the popular thoughts and feelings of the time. Watching Alan's last film, you saw the subject of football hooliganism transformed with characteristic wit and grace, yet without any of the cosmetic prettiness customary to television. It was shocking, of course, but shocking only because it was true. Even after *The Firm*, the club struck back, at once staging an immediate post-screening discussion – a sort of whoops-too-late prophylactic health warning about what you shouldn't have been watching earlier. The only two people in Britain immune to the film's power – sociologists, inevitably, from Leicester – agreed with a man in a suit from Next that we had seen it all before. Another BBC controller was wheeled out, this time to tell us, in the well-worn catchphrase of his profession, that the cuts he had made in the film were not censorship, they were editorial control.

A wave of sentiment has followed on Alan's death, and rightly, for he was a man as worthy of love and admiration as any most of us have known. But a special grief seems to follow on the death of those who embody virtues of which we ourselves feel the need to be reminded and which we wish to hold in common. Alan knew better than anyone that cultural organisations ought to exist to serve the public and the artist, not to mediate between them. Never, in all these apparently pointless struggles, did Alan lose his fathomless good humour. Nor was he deflected from his aim of creating some of the most original and interesting television of his time. The club has lost its most distinguished non-member.

The Separation of Wheel and Track

In 2003 the Guardian *magazine asked me for an introduction to the play* The Permanent Way, *which was about
to open in the old railway town of York before setting off
on a long tour of England. The railways interested me as
an example of the many admittedly difficult problems to
which the political class, almost alone, is determined to
give the worst available answer.*

When, a few years ago, word was going round of the plan
to persist with a massive millennium project on a riverside
site down Greenwich way, the theatre producer Cameron
Mackintosh (*Cats, Les Miserables*) was approached by
a prominent Labour minister who invited him to lend
his expertise. The impresario reacted in honest bewilderment. 'You mean you're planning to open an £800
million Dome in eighteen months' time and, as of today,
you haven't the slightest idea what you're planning to
put in it?' Mackintosh refused the gig, adding that if the
Dome had been a show of his, he would have started
preparing for it ten years previously.

There is, I suppose, a grisly fascination in seeing elected
politicians blunder into situations from which any normal

person would walk instantly away. (The popular term for such incidents is, by the way, 'train crashes'.) The whole experience of being a sentient adult in the Western world in 2003 has involved being forced to stand to one side, watching in disbelief, while the governments of two English-speaking countries undertook massively unpopular policies with exactly the consequences which all intelligent bystanders foresaw – civil chaos in Iraq, the worsening of prospects for peace in the Middle East, and the inevitable undermining of international law. As this errantly peculiar and disturbing year has gone on, there have been two over-riding questions dominating the voters' attitude to politics, to neither of which has any very satisfactory answer yet been given: why are we increasingly witnessing circumstances in which – maybe from a cocktail of credulousness, special interest, and ignorance – politicians embark on courses which everyone else can see in advance to be fatally flawed? And, more pressingly, what the hell can we do about it?

If you, or a member of your family, have not been its direct victim, then the privatisation of the railways may seem to have been an error of judgement with small consequences compared, for example, with the 100,000 deaths inflicted by the refusal of George Bush and Tony Blair to give Hans Blix the six months he needed to complete his altogether excellent and subsequently vindicated work. The number of fatalities directly attributable to the dismantling of our publicly-owned, publicly run railway is, after all, deeply contentious. Some people are even ready to argue that all those foreigners and commuters might have been killed anyway. And their families, they say, might have been treated just as contemptuously by the old authorities as the families of the victims of Southall, Ladbroke Grove and Potters Bar have been by the new. But there is, beyond doubt, in the story of how British Rail was first auctioned off at bargain prices, to the fourfold profit of the City of London, a painful parable about the badness of British government. And in the failure of the following Labour administration to address the roots of the problem it inherited you may also learn something instructive about the disconnection now so apparent between the political class and the people they were once supposed to be serving.

Everyone in Britain wants a cheap and effective railway. And yet for the nine months during which I have been researching my play *The Permanent Way* and talking to people involved at almost every level of the operation, I have not been able to find one single person – not one – willing to defend the overall form of the original privatisation. There are admittedly a few people who can still see nothing wrong in principle with the costly brainwave of separating wheel and track. It may be apparent to you and to every other casual user of the railroad that putting one profit-seeking company in charge of the line and another profit-seeking company in charge of the trains was always likely to lead to astronomical increases in cost and inefficiency – matched, of course, by disastrous effects on safety. But some people, most of them inside the Treasury, do still cling to the fantasy – now almost Austin Powers-like in its period appeal – that competition, in however unsuitable a context, must of itself be a good thing. There are also, to be fair, some optimistic and hardworking souls inside the industry who believe in amelioration. They see Network Rail's recent decision at least to take maintenance, if not renewal, back in-house as a late step in the right direction. But there is no one – I repeat no one – who does not believe that the legislation which was laid out in the Railways Act of 1993 was so fundamentally misconceived as to be effectively unworkable. And – yet more shocking – there is no one who does not, from one point of view or another, confess that they knew this equally well at the time.

Hindsight has been a popular word in 2003, and you might think it is being employed again when experts tell you of John Major's need to demonstrate political continuity with Margaret Thatcher by forcing through 'one more privatisation'. Poll Tax Peggy did not, as popularly believed, disdain to privatise the railways because she disliked them. Far more practical, she did not want them put in private hands because she did not see how they could make money. She, at least, could see that capitalism is driven by profit. Where, she asked, with some prescience, was honest profit to be found in the railways? But even if we are able confidently to dismiss Major's balkanisation – the operation was split, remember, into 113 parts – as the barmy ideological spluttering of a weak Prime Minister desperate to fake strength, what are we to make, then, of an incoming Labour cabinet which fought that balkanisation as hard as it could in opposition, but which then refused, on the first day of office in 1997, to do anything effective or radical to reverse it?

You may, at one level, be amused to remember Tony Blair describing railway privatisation on 23 March 1995 as 'absurd'. You may respect a leader of the Opposition who remarks that the Conservatives 'want to replace a comprehensive, co-ordinated railway network with a hotchpotch of private companies linked together by a gigantic bureaucratic paperchase of contracts – overseen of course by a clutch on quangos'. You may wholeheartedly agree when he adds that, 'As the public learn more about the chaos and cost, their anger at this folly will grow.' But what possible respect can you retain for a man who believes that a proposition which was self-evident when he was on one set of green benches has somehow ceased to be self-evident, for the sole reason that he himself has in the meantime won an election? How can something be true one day and not the next, solely because 'I' have been elected to a club? There is, to say the very least, in this particular shift of perspective something deeply illuminating about the reasons why, right across the country and across a whole range of issues, voters feel that it is *only* politicians who cannot see what is bleeding obvious to the rest of us. Everyone knows. The railways should have been renationalised, or, at the very least, reintegrated, on the first day of Labour's access to power.

Of all the interviews which the actors of the Out of Joint Company and I have conducted, none perhaps has been more striking than that with an investment banker who was intimately involved with the original flotation, and who watched Railtrack deliberately drive their share price up in two years, from the offer price of £3.90 to a gut-busting £17.58. I asked him at what point he realised things were going wrong, not in the City but on the railways themselves. 'Well,' he said, 'I do remember on the morning of the Ladbroke Grove crash, I did think, this separation of wheel and track ain't good.' The banker then added thoughtfully: 'I don't think the basic idea was a mistake, but on the other hand I would have to admit that at every episode since privatisation, something bizarre has happened. And that does make you ask: is it the structure? It seems not fit for the purpose.'

Plainly, it is not in the character of many successful bankers to draw attention to the shortcomings of schemes from which they themselves have done well. So there was something moving to me in the honestly expressed doubt of a man who can now see that the venture which once caused him such a professional rush ('I love flotation') had, in fact, also been the cause of considerable suffering to large numbers of people. In that phrase 'not fit for purpose', the banker was facing the central point which has run like a thread of steel through all our research: because privatisation was conceived wrong, it can never work. By putting the manager and the paper-pusher in the space once occupied by the engineer, the railways have become almost as dangerous as they are expensive. And yet, once more, the response any fair-minded observer has to such frankness is to ask why there remains only one category of person resolutely unwilling to draw the lessons from this kind of honesty. As of today, the subsidy given by the taxpayer is more than three times what it was before the railways were privatised. What on earth is stopping *only* politicians from drawing the democratic conclusion? Why was something said to be 'inefficient' when it was half the price and considerably less lethal? Why is it said to be 'efficient' solely because it is in private hands? And is it the government's sly hope that the moral horror occasioned by a repellent company like Jarvis ceases to be a matter of public concern, simply because the railways are no longer technically 'public'?

All over the world this year, we see the same phenomenon of electorates waiting, bewildered or furious, for their own leaders to catch up with them, and trying to understand the mystery of their refusal. During the Iraq war, I was given a quotation from Eisenhower – a soldier, and a brave one too – who observed in the 1950s: 'I think that people want peace so much that one of these days government had better get out of the way and let them have it.' It's strange. For the early part of my lifetime the rebuke repeatedly offered to anyone not professionally engaged in politics was that they were able to go on harbouring an unrealistic (or idealistic) view of human nature. They were told all the time that they were licensed to dream, because unlike politicians or businessmen, they were not forced to face the ugly facts about the real motivations of human beings. Yet somehow in the last few years the position has flipped dramatically. Now it is *only* the political class, here and in the US, who become roguishly excited when setting off on ridiculous and impractical schemes, based on wild, unprovable beliefs: 'If we launch an illegal invasion of Iraq, democracy will catch on throughout the Middle East'; 'If we give the Israelis *carte blanche* to bash the living hell out of the Palestinians, the Palestinians will eventually give in'; 'If we introduce competition on the railways, the service will improve.' Now, in comparison with the *in situ* peddlers of busted dreams, the people themselves appear hard-headed and practical. My impression is that nobody except George Bush wanted the UN undermined. Neither my Israeli nor my Palestinian friends want the terrorist nihilism of Ariel Sharon and the suicide bombers. And everybody – yes, everybody – wants the railways vertically reintegrated.

Above all, I think, people are becoming tired of being lectured by the Prime Minister that there is no effective alternative to a cowardly Labour government. They know there is. It's a courageous Labour government.

The Second Intifada

The shadow of the Iraq invasion, the most contentious and divisive event in British history since the Suez adventure of 1956, inevitably falls over some of the last essays in this book. By the early summer of 2002, as the lethal unreason and opportunism of the American government's reaction to the attack on the World Trade Centre was starting to come clear, I had decided to accept an invitation to revive Via Dolorosa *for a summer season in the West End of London. My reasons were given in this article.*

When I concluded my New York theatre debut by leaving the Booth Theater and walking away down Schubert Alley on a hot Sunday night in June 1999, at the end of a sometimes exhausting, sometimes exhilarating four-month run, I must admit I had little idea that only three years later, I would be once more be contemplating an actor's life. It's the last thing I had in mind. I had taken to the stage in the first place only because a visit to Israel and the Palestinian Territory had left me despairing of any other means of conveying the vividness of my reactions except by direct address. I felt, for this one subject only, I had no alternative but to stand in a theatre in person and forgo the playwright's usual convenient cover of hiring specialists who will do the speaking for him.

The director Stephen Daldry and I had planned a play which we had expected would probably play only to an esoteric public for a few performances in the Theatre Upstairs. But even when it slowly became apparent that we were answering in larger audiences of all ages, races and backgrounds an unexpected demand for an evening which took one step back from the violent passions of Jew and Arab – which sought, above all, to illuminate rather than to persuade – it still seemed unlikely that we would ever feel the need to perform the play again. People were kind enough to tell us, sometimes, it seemed, with rather more surprise than admiration, that we had taken the Broadway play about as far away as it could go from its more familiar fascination with the domestic family and its privileged dysfunctions. But it hardly occurred to us that in such a short time a revival of *Via Dolorosa* might seem even more urgent.

Since the beginning of the second intifada in September 2000, it has been the fate of any writer who is known to be interested in the Middle East regularly to be invited to make some sort of public statement about the rights and wrongs of the latest developments in the conflict. Since 11 September, scarcely a day goes by in which some glib questionnaire does not drop through a writer's door asking him or her to take sides, to explain in just one hundred words ('by e-mail, please' they always say) why they personally do or do not approve of the particular actions of particular governments – as if profound questions of power and faith could somehow be dispatched to the historical boundary by the flick of a novelist's wrist. The campaigning journalist John Pilger has argued that it reveals the endemic poverty of British cultural life that so few writers of fiction have been willing to rush into print to swing their supposed weight behind one side or another in any of the current global upheavals. In his view, it shows a dismaying lack of literary interest in politics. But if my own thinking is at all representative, then this uncommon display of writerly modesty has argued to the contrary. It is precisely because I think of myself as being so deeply, almost hopelessly interested in politics that I have been nervous of adding anything unconsidered to the recent popular carnival of opinion.

In saying this, it's important to make clear my proper respect for those who make a professional living out of expressing their views – or rather for those lucky few who are actually good at it. The astonishingly full and fair-minded reports of a superb correspondent like Suzanne Goldenberg in the *Guardian* have only been deepened by the work of first-rate analysts like David Hirst. And it would also be true to say that, in private, I have scarcely lacked for colourful opinions of my own. It would, God knows, be an unnaturally hard-hearted or brutal soul who could contemplate the needless mutual slaughter of the last twenty-one months (as I write, at least 2,150 people killed, 1,600 of them Palestinian, 550 Israeli), who could look at the photographs of Israeli families destroyed by the murderous tactics of the 71 so-called 'suicide bombers' or at the horrifying pictures of innocent Palestinians caught up in the path of a military subjugation which brings them nothing but yet more suffering and oppression, without spontaneously calling down judgement or instantly proclaiming a heartfelt curse on one faction or another. Surely, when moved, I believe I can make my voice heard in the saloon bar as well as the next man. But every time I have found myself shouting at the television, either to refute the callous and unfeeling evasions of Israeli cabinet spokesmen, or to recoil at the morbid triumphalism of those anti-Zionists who seem happy to use loss of young life as evidence of success, then I have found myself making a noise which, even to my own ears, sounds more than a little bit thin and forced. I am haunted by the undignified feeling that this is somehow not what I am best at.

Those of us who supported the American action in Afghanistan, not only as a legitimate act of self-defence but also as a humanitarian undertaking on behalf of a country desperately in need of relief, enjoyed a brief moment of hope last autumn when we thought we detected the evidence of a welcome seriousness in US foreign policy. For those few weeks at least, we were able to believe the West had rediscovered its role. The Bush administration, and in particular, our own Prime Minister, both seemed to think it a new and urgent priority, in the wake of the World Trade Centre attack, to consider again what influence could be brought to bear by outside parties to build on the faltering but important progress occasioned by the Oslo accords. Commentators rushed to assure us that in a new mood of regretful self-examination, Americans were willing once more to take up the burden of playing a full and proper part in international affairs. But as time has gone by, and the first impact of that invasion of American territory has faded, so too has any discernible sense of exterior purpose or direction in the actions of its government.

When, some months ago, George Bush announced that it was now official US policy to commit itself to the establishment of a sovereign Palestinian state, then it seemed reasonable to accept that this was an offer which the President was making in good faith, and that he had indeed learnt the lessons of his own initial reluctance to use America's power to intervene in the region. It was also natural to assume that Bush had in mind some practical plan for how this new state might one day be brought about. But if you have watched the pitifully weak, almost humiliating behaviour of the US in the last six months, as it has stood to one side and permitted the abuse of military power to wreck the lives of peaceable citizens in both territories, then you will be left, like me, with an unpleasant feeling of having been suckered.

Against the opinion of many of my closest friends, I believed in the correctness of the first American interventions in Afghanistan because its administration, in a genuine state of shock, promised that it would henceforth be interested not just in defending the personal safety of those born into the world's richest nations, but in developing some more enlightened attitude to its poorest. That promise appears to have been rescinded. The latest risible speech by the President on 24 June, in which he counselled that the future lay with one of the two principal parties to the conflict electing itself a new leader, offered plenty of spurious moral exhortation, but absolutely no vision, no timetable and no concrete plan. (As one American official, more honest than his President, remarked, 'How we move this forward, when everyone's spoken to it, is still not clear to me.') It seems more and more as if a venture which started out as a commendable moral crusade in defence of freedom has ended up as nothing but a particularly squalid and inept campaign to re-elect the President. Colin Powell, who promised so much, has delivered precisely nothing. Add to that: I have been startled to realise, by the swaggeringly stupid pronouncements of cabinet members like Condoleezza Rice and Donald Rumsfeld that the prevailing US foreign policy view of the Middle East – barely caricatured as good guys v. bad guys – is not just ignorant of the roots and causes of all the important divisions in the area. Worse, it is boastfully ignorant.

In these circumstances nobody is going to pretend that the revival of a mere stage play will, or could, make a blind bit of difference to what has become a terrifying international debacle. How can it? At all the original outings of *Via Dolorosa*, the people most conspicuous by their absence from the auditorium were, predictably, Western politicians. No doubt, they all regard themselves as so brilliantly informed that they don't need to waste ninety-five minutes listening to anyone. But the fact is that, as a writer, I am lost for any *other* way to react.

Chekhov wrote that people were entitled at all times to two basic freedoms: the freedom from violence and the freedom from lies. Self-evidently, most of us are powerless to do anything about the first. Like everyone else, I am sitting at home, watching the situation deteriorate and wondering, day by day, how it can possibly get worse. But about the second freedom – the freedom from lies – I can at least do a little. In a situation in which barely any partisan seems capable of statements untainted by misrepresentation (Ariel Sharon recently achieved the dazzling feat of a thousand-word article in the *New York Times* which purported to be a fifty-year history of Palestinian–Israeli relations but which did not once mention the word 'occupation'), then the one very small thing I can do is put back on public display a work whose original intention, at least, was to express some specific, unpartisan truths.

It was, in fact, at the beginning of this year that I agreed to the experiment of giving two charity readings of *Via Dolorosa* in Sydney, Australia. I was there for the performance of another of my plays at Neil Armfield's famous Belvoir Street Theatre. It would, Neil argued, at least give Australians a chance to hear the author read a work they might otherwise miss. And if it was dated, so what? As the author, however, I was all too well aware that my play, written at the beginning of 1998, was the fruit of what seems in retrospect like a period of comparative calm. It described a moment, if not of peace, then at least of wary stability. More important, it took testimony from a time when people still believed, admittedly to a diminishing extent, that education, co-operation and cultural exchange might have a role to play in Israeli–Palestinian relations. In those days, it was not uncommon to hear people say that if only the children from either side could be regularly brought together in friendship, then a new generation could grow up free of the hatreds that had ruined the lives of their parents and of their parents' parents.

You did not need to be deeply in touch with the hardening of attitudes in the Middle East to know that this moment of romantic open-mindedness was long past. After the failure of the 2000 Camp David talks, the Left in Israel had abdicated its positions, eagerly selling the pass and permitting the fanatics and the expansionists to portray all leading Palestinian politicians as racially untrustworthy. ('Arabs,' said Ehud Barak, 'lie.') In Palestine, Arafat had tolerated and even encouraged the hopeless delusion that a second intifada, this time characterised by actions of the vilest inhumanity, could somehow recover the moral and practical authority of the first. Both sides were ruthlessly committed to doomed policies – one to a fantasy that it was possible for a colonial power to guarantee security purely for its own citizens without making even the most grudging move towards offering justice to the colonised; the other, to the delusion that it was ever going to be seen as either heroic or acceptable to use indiscriminate murder as a tactic of progress. From behind the barricades of these untenable positions, from which neither side was being offered any outside impetus to escape, there was always going to be a danger that my poor play would look both naive and ingenuous.

It remains for the audience at the Duchess Theatre to decide whether *Via Dolorosa*, unchanged word for word from its original production, still bears successful witness to the complexity of the hopes and beliefs of so many individuals who meanwhile wish to be allowed to get on with their lives. The play's basic strategy is to offer people from all points of view the chance to speak for themselves, and to explain the reasoning behind their most profound historical or spiritual convictions. All I can report from Australia, after two nerve-racking evenings a few weeks ago, is that it seemed, at least from where I was standing, that this approach was now, if anything, more refreshing than ever. After so much heat, everyone appeared to welcome the chance to enjoy a little cool. I had resolved in advance to perform the original text, to make no fake or cosmetic pretence that the play was more up-to-date than it was. But, interestingly, this decision to permit the attitudes of four years ago to gain perspective from the passage of events – to allow, as it were, some air to blow around them – did nothing but add depth to the evening. Some characters, in particular Benny Begin, the one time Minister of Science in Netanyahu's government, came across as eerily prescient. Others seemed tragic because they have already been left behind by history.

Not entirely by coincidence, London theatregoers will have the chance to compare the sober reportage of an ageing European with a far more authentic and pressing account of life under the occupation. Last year the Al-

Kasaba Theatre Company, whose artistic director George Ibrahim is one of the characters in my play, presented its wonderful show *Alive from Palestine* for a ridiculously short run organised, again, by the Royal Court, and mounted as part of the London International Festival of Theatre. The immediate acclaim afforded to the company ('The most life-changing experience in drama this year': *The Independent*), and the impossibility of anyone getting in to see them, has meant that a group of charitable British artists, including Vanessa Redgrave, Caryl Churchill, Stephen Daldry, Richard Curtis, Nick Hornby and Julia Ormond have clubbed together to sponsor their return, this time to the Young Vic from 18 to 27 July, in the hope that a wider audience might be able to hear for themselves exactly what it's been like living under the cosh of recent events. Nothing seems to me more important than the chance to hear directly from the victims of the present violence at a length, and sometimes with a breadth, which journalism can only sometimes achieve.

Those who examine the small print above and below the titles of *Via Dolorosa* and *Alive from Palestine* will not be surprised to notice that both these projects – which are deliberately being presented at the same time – have been developed by Elyse Dodgson's international department at the Royal Court. This unassuming tributary of the old powerhouse's mainstream programme has already proved itself earlier this year in its Russian and Middle Eastern seasons to be one of the liveliest and most important sources of drama in London. In a curious article in the *Guardian* three months ago, at the most recent height of hostilities, the columnist Ian Buruma asked why it was that the Israel-Palestine dispute had such a powerful hold over the imagination of the Western middle classes. Why did passions run so high among people who were apparently not even directly involved? He went on to suggest that our identification with the problems of the area came primarily out of a desire to exorcise our own guilt. How do I reply? Truthfully, Buruma would do well to buy tickets for both these upcoming plays. My own belief is that human beings will always be interested in questions of faith. And never more so than when faith is in collision with justice.

Chardonnay on the Potomac

Not long after Saddam's statue had been toppled in Baghdad, it became clear that a massive effort would now be made by the British and American governments, and by their supporters in the press, to help them accelerate away from the moral implications of their own actions. In this article from June 2003 are the seeds of the conviction which would go on to inform the writing of Stuff Happens, *a play about the diplomatic process leading up to the war. Bush, the supposedly stupid man, was getting everything he wanted: Blair, the clever man, nothing.*

'When I try to understand what's going on every morning, I tell myself there's been a military coup.'

American diplomat

One of my favourite literary jokes of the last twenty years was made when a well-known novelist, hitherto apolitical, announced that the recent birth of his first baby had convinced him that he could not tolerate living in a world which contained nuclear weapons. The critic Adam Mars-Jones responded by noting that he had heard many

powerful and convincing arguments both for and against
the bomb, but that his final judgement on the question
was unlikely to be swayed by the fact that Martin Amis
had recently become a father.

The same potential for epic self-importance attends all
those of us who have found the last period of international conflict among the most seriously disillusioning
of our lives. We risk making fools of ourselves. Frankly,
you may ask, who cares? It would, after all, be a rare
idiot who had followed the direction of our last two
governments and imagined that their leaders gave a hoot,
private or public, for the thoughts and feelings of those
who had argued or even campaigned for their election.
Blair and Brown claim in their rhetoric not to be victims
of the traditional deformities of the Left. But, curiously,
for all their talk of breaking the bonds of the past, they
have both inherited one of the Left's most disabling char-
acteristics. They continue to show much more vigour
when finding fault with their friends than they do when
giving stick to their enemies. Any plain citizen – anyone,
in fact, ruled rather than ruling – would have to be blind
with conceit not to notice that the Blair–Brown project
has motored forwards on a powerful fuel made up of
two parts admiration for the opposition mixed with three
parts contempt for their own supporters.

What does it matter, then, if those of us who have
always believed in social democracy now find ourselves
seized by a unique, impotent sense of shame at the collu-
sion of a British government in a manifestly cooked-up
invasion of a foreign country? When, a few months ago,

I wrote in a newspaper about an illegal occupation which was predicated on at least five principal untruths (1, that Iraq represented a threat to the United States; 2, that it presented a current or increased threat to its neighbours; 3, that it had developed nuclear weapons; 4, that it was linked in any way to Al Qaeda and to the devastation of 11 September; and 5, that Hans Blix was being fooled, through his own ingenuousness, in what turned out, in reality, to be his scrupulous and thorough searches for chemical and biological weapons), then I was properly rebuked by correspondents asking why I was so ready to press the case against the US, and yet had, apparently, not a word of blame for my own government. It was a fair question. It was also hard to reply.

My fault, but alongside an apparently small minority of my fellow countrymen: I have always been instinctively sympathetic to domestic politicians. It had long seemed to me that many of them, and most obviously those in left-wing parties, were people willing to take on problems which most of us find easier to leave alone. My experience in 1993 of being given access to watch Neil Kinnock at close quarters throughout his doomed attempt to become Prime Minister left me markedly intolerant of people who love to declare that anyone standing for election must necessarily be a fool or a crook. It seemed even sillier, as Fleet Street does, to seek first to elevate individual politicians and then, through an inevitable cycle of attrition and fatigue – a kind of boring media war – always to consign them to a place where they are deemed no longer worthy of the journalistic community's high standards.

My own belief in the difficulty and desirability of democratic politics was hardly based on a utopian view of what might be achieved. Just as important, I could reluctantly see that most Western societies were made up of people and interest groups who wanted very different things. They could not all be satisfied at the same time. Whereas most of us could airily wave a leader-writer's hand and proclaim, 'This should be done – and then this,' without actually having to follow through the practical implications of what we urged, politicians were the poor mugs who were allocated the job of reconciling the irreconcilable. In our own lives, most of us habitually equivocated, elided, jumped logic, changed our minds and generally faffed about on the margins of conviction. But it was only politicians whose profession obliged them to be held to account for these particular offences.

When I heard some stray minister being roasted in Parliament for a chance remark he had unwittingly made five years previously, I would wince in sympathy and think how few of my own utterances would survive this kind of examination. If politicians dodged, weaved and buckled language to a point where it screamed for mercy ('I did not have sexual relations with that woman') then it was, in part, because their trade committed them to higher levels of scrupulousness than the rest of us. They were under scrutiny. A lot of us aren't. Watching all the hallmark sweating and wriggling of the professional pol, I was usually persuaded of Fawn Brodie's pronouncement: 'There's a little bit of Richard Nixon in all of us.' Only on occasions did I tend instead towards

John Kenneth Galbraith's equally memorable riposte: 'I say, the hell there is.'

It is difficult therefore for someone of my temperament to accept that my own feelings about politicians have become worse than irrelevant. They have become worthless. Why? Because local politicians are, definitively, no longer speaking to me. The important dialogue in Britain is no longer carried on between the governors and the governed, but is maintained in another direction entirely: neither up nor down, but east–west, between the colony and the imperial capital. The charge has been made – as though it were the most damning possible – that Britain and America decided to annex Iraq and then afterwards searched for any random justification, however implausible, which they could find to decorate their intentions. (Paul Wolfowitz's own words plainly bear that meaning, and Clare Short is telling us the same). But far more troubling, at least to those of us who imagine that some sort of national conversation still goes on, is the knowledge that it is now impossible to imagine *any* American foreign policy, however irrational, however dangerous, however illegal, with which our present Prime Minister would not declare himself publicly delighted and thrilled.

These are, it is clear, frightening times. A revolutionary doctrine of the pre-emptive strike has been introduced into international relations, but its use is to be privileged for one country only, on no other grounds but that this particularly country is so powerful as to be beyond sanction. The UN, which was established, in Samantha

Power's words, 'specifically to end the days of military intervention dressed up as humanitarianism' has been pushed brutally to the side. From now on, America will do what it damn well pleases, but the messy business of explaining and justifying will be left largely to the junior partner. Harold Wilson is held in history to be the most untrustworthy and wily practitioner of the black arts of politics, yet even he managed the principled feat of remaining allied to Lyndon Johnson without uselessly killing British soldiers in a similarly doubtful venture. If, as Stanley Kubrick claimed, large states often behave like gangsters while small states often behave like prostitutes, then we may at least console ourselves that we have descended to a point where we are more whore than racketeer. But the sum effect is to leave us in a world where no one will listen to us. They know we have voluntarily surrendered our wish for an independent voice in foreign affairs. Worse, we have surrendered it to a country which is actively seeking to undermine international organisations and international law. Lacking the gun, we are to be only the mouth. The deal is this: America provides the firepower. We provide the bullshit.

The easy thing, of course, in response to this *fait accompli* is to hand all discourse back to the cynics and to say that the deeply impressive massed ranks of two million voters in February indeed represented, as the Labour government hoped, nothing but a walk in the park. As the Americans lie back on their Roman pillows and toy insincerely with a laughable road map for the Middle East which is touted, among other things, as

Tony Blair's reward for his loyalty, and which, in a world now pathologically distrustful of American intentions, has no conceivable chance of success, the temptation is to throw our hands up and declare that there is no alternative but for the rest of us to join our short-sleeved cousins lolling in the bleachers. We are to watch as innocent people spin to their deaths, whether in Gaza, on the West Bank or in Tel Aviv. The status quo of occupation and chaos in Afghanistan and Iraq and of savage butchery in the Palestinian Territory and Israel is already acquiring a disturbingly permanent look. Summer is coming, the weather is changing on the Potomac and in the Home Counties, and you can feel, as our rulers reach for the barbecue forks and the Chardonnay, as they gather forgivingly again for their *frotteurs'* trade union meetings in Evian – 'How lovely to see you, Mr Bush', 'No, how lovely to see *you*' – a growing confidence that although something utterly dishonourable happened in public life earlier this year, there is no reason that, like all dishonourable things, it should not soon be forgotten.

Well, there it is. Those of us who opposed the war from the start have won the argument and lost all influence. Even if we are unwise, as I think we are, to focus our vindication on the fruitless ninety-six-day search for weapons of mass destruction – the war was *wrong*, it was wrong regardless, because it was outside the authority of the United Nations – nevertheless we are left at the end of it all in the curious position of finding no satisfaction or purpose in our own rightness. The policies are not going to change. We are going to be ignored. In the aftermath of an invasion which is now recognised all over the world to have been conceived, born and carried out in mendacity, we have, it seems, only one obligation, and it is one which may one day even provide our shivering democracy with a useful antibiotic. It is to set out and nail the remaining lies which the belligerent are still trying to advance for their cover.

Of these the most important and insidious is the idea, given much romantic play, particularly in Europe, that Americans are, by nature, isolated from the rest of the world and therefore charmingly incompetent at the exercise of diplomacy. This seems to me the exact opposite of the truth. It may well have been useful to the pursuit of recent US policy to pretend that there is still some element of prairie innocence at large on Capitol Hill. Implicitly, the question is put: 'How can we homespun regular folk be expected to find our way through these damned complicated international organisations?' But the disastrous mistake, on our side of the argument, has been to indulge this American exceptionalism for even one moment. Whatever the patronising propaganda emanating from Downing Street – 'Yes, the Americans are a bit crude, but, don't worry, we'll smooth things over' – there is nothing peculiar to the American character which exempts it from the obligations of diplomacy. On the contrary. For an administration which is widely held to be provincially ignorant of the world, you may notice that it is doing remarkably well at getting its way in it.

It may be perfect fun to crack our sides at the witty anti-war campaigner who claims that 'God invented war to teach the Americans geography.' But we should be aware that when we do so, we play straight into the war-makers' hands. It suits them better than they can tell. They love it when we choose to assume that they are rough and artless, even naive. The truth is, it isn't likely. The more plausible interpretation is that they know exactly where they're going. When Colin Powell walks out of the General Assembly in a snit because he believes a Frenchman has been rude to him, it is not, as he would claim, because he has tried very hard to be reasonable, but dammit, there is a limit; it is because he is deliberately using diplomatic incompetence as an excuse for the US to thenceforward be licensed to do exactly as it chooses. If it wished, America could perfectly well do as its critics advise and 'grow up'. It could easily engage with the world's arguments against it. Why not? It wouldn't be hard. It is, oddly, a mark of our own stupidity that we seem incapable of grasping the point that the US does not engage for the simple reason that it does not want to – any more than President Bush wants to take notice of unthinking liberals who keep advising him to 'travel more'.

The overriding offence of all of us in Europe, on whatever side of the argument, has been to have peddled the notion that because President Bush is inarticulate, he must therefore be stupid. It is a peculiarly English snobbery and it is damaging. Anyone who has read the high-wire Darwinism of Stephen Pinker would know that an inability competently to handle language does not argue a lack of coherent purpose or intention. We can laugh as much as we wish at slogans like 'The moron's got a war on'. We can even buy *Private Eye* and indulge its falsely comforting view of a man who is too dumb to know how many beans make five. We may, like Tony Blair himself, elevate our own importance, we may parlay our world role by managing to imply that we are acting as a restraining influence on these hopeless barbarians. (To a friend who said that he was grateful that Tony Blair had been in the room when some of the recent discussions had gone on in the White House, the Prime Minister replied that only those who had been in the room could have any idea just how wild some of those discussions had been.) But when we do so, we miss the larger facts and we mistake our analysis. Consider. At the end of the war, Bush has rising popularity, a cowed and craven media which has abandoned all serious pretensions to investigation or even to basic reporting, and a Democratic opposition which has been triumphantly blackmailed into nervous, pseudo-patriotic silence. Meanwhile, he is raising money, hand over fist, for his own coronation. Blair has falling popularity, the media on his neck, and may never be trusted again. The Labour Party, by report, is not expanding. Which one clever? Which one stupid?

When Shall We Live?

This, the eleventh Eric Symes Abbot Memorial Lecture, was delivered at Westminster Abbey on 9 May 1996 and then, on the day after, at Keble College, Oxford. It was an unusual commission, but its arguments were taken sufficiently seriously for the speaker the following year to spend a good part of his lecture rebutting me. It is a mark of the character of the start of the twenty-first century that the open mind of the Anglican Church already feels more attractive, and more like strength, than it did a few years ago.

Although, for me, it is plainly a great privilege to be asked to give this year's Eric Symes Abbot Memorial lecture, I can well understand if there are those among you who are contemplating the choice of the present speaker with a certain bewilderment. I must admit that as I prepared to speak, I have shared a good deal of that bewilderment myself. The Church of England is distinguished by its exceptionally non-doctrinaire and generous attitude to those who do not share its own most sacred beliefs. For better or worse, it is nothing if it is not a liberal church. But even so, I can see that it is quite striking that the

Dean of Westminster should invite an obvious heathen to speak in memory of a man who, from what I have read of him, seems chiefly marked out from other men by the power of his Christian faith and example.

The oddness of the invitation does not stop there. Westminster Abbey is what is called a Royal Peculiar. That means that it is not under the jurisdiction of any Bishop. Least of all, I was told, in a tone which betrayed an almost Trollopian intensity of feeling, is it, God forbid, under the authority of the Bishop of London. The Queen herself is technically known as the Abbey's Visitor. But it is as a wholehearted, even slightly obsessive republican that I stand here, making my remarks in a church which, even for me, is most movingly full of the evidence of its own intimate connections with monarchs, living and dead. Those of us who believe and have long argued that the hacking death-rattle of royalty is obscuring other, more positive noises in Great Britain are well used to the abuse we attract from our impassioned opponents. Yet even I was intrigued by the line of attack taken against us in a recent edition of the *Guardian*. The article had started with the routine attempts to type enemies of the Palace as embittered no-hopers, themselves intent on taking over the running of the country and crazed by the heady prospect of drinking their kir and eating their olives with their literary cronies on the balcony of Buckingham Palace. But as the journalist went on, he reported a rather more interesting argument and one which served to bring me up short. The entertaining royalist historian Andrew Roberts, whose book about the followers of Churchill I admired as much as anyone, was reported as saying that there was one crucial difference between monarchists and republicans, a difference which indicated to any honest observer which side must finally be in the right: that whereas monarchists were, as a group, willing to die for their beliefs, republicans plainly weren't.

In saying this, of course, Roberts was trying to establish that constitutional reform of any kind is a concern of what the press in its most self-hating and exhausted cliché likes to call 'the chattering classes'. Faith in the Queen, Roberts implied, was in some way a true emotion, whereas faith in democracy must, by contrast, be a phoney one. But it seemed to me an odd way for an historian to vindicate his own case, and indeed one which might unintentionally put him in some distinctly dubious company. Active service members of the IRA, wreaking their random bombings on the city streets, are, after all, willing to die for their beliefs. The fighters of Hamas, who murder women and children in Jerusalem, are willing to die for their beliefs. Japanese kamikazes, firing killer sprays on the Tokyo underground, are willing to die for their beliefs. I began at once to form the picture of a portly young historian with barrels of dynamite tied round his chest, going to blow himself up at a meeting of Charter 88, and all in the interests of defending the uneasy House of Windsor.

Beneath this happy image lies what I hope is an important idea, and one which I intend to provide the starting point of this lecture: that most of us, indeed, do have little idea of what we believe, and are also extremely confused on the subject of whether we would be willing to die for it. Somewhere, in nearly every theological volume I have read, it is asserted that the most important decision any person has to make on earth is what form of supreme being he or she does or does not believe in. Yet the mystery of this supposedly urgent subject is just how many days, weeks, or indeed years so many of us pass quite contentedly without once being troubled by it. Although you might feel the question of God's nature and existence ought to be obsessively important to each and every one of us, the simple fact of the modern world is that it is not felt to be. At least until the approach of death, the majority of Westerners are willing to tick the box in which they profess that they have some generalised religious belief but they are jiggered if they can actually say what it is.

This is, at first glance, a peculiar state of affairs. It is also one for which I do not think the conventional explanations quite hold water. The usual means of arguing away the modern indifference to conventional religion is to assert that because we in the West may expect to live longer than we used to, and because we endure less physical suffering, we have therefore lost some crucial sense of what life is actually about. In the Middle Ages, it is said, death was all around. People had an inborn sense of how transitory their existence was. They knew they were not here for long. For that reason their minds were wonderfully focused on the question of where they might be going next. They also knew the unspeakable horror of unrelieved pain and the sharp cruelty of sudden death. So they had no problem, it is said, in directing their minds towards a place where human loss might be explained and, hopefully, relieved. But now, it is argued, comfort and even luxury have inured us to considering the shortness and harshness of our span on earth. The soothing apparatus of our hospitals, the bright lights in our shopping malls, the constant chatter of our television sets and the general anaesthetic prosperity of our surroundings all combine to protect us from brute physical unpleasantness, which was once such a powerful spur to religious fear, if not to religious understanding.

I must say I have some difficulty with this argument. Like many people, I find it hard to admire a God who feels the need to make life short and brutal in order for His creation to appreciate Him better. I have my doubts about a religious faith which depends on human deprivation and hardship for it to achieve a suitable intensity. If the only way we can be moved to believe in God is by experiencing the very worst aspects of the world He has created, I have very grave difficulties with what kind of God He must therefore be. If human beings are, as Christianity claims, put on this earth to worship God and to do His will, it seems an extraordinary state of affairs that they should need to be reminded of that purpose only by the bitterness and brevity of their own lives.

The other way, of course, that the Church consoles itself for the apparent lack of interest in its own affairs is by asserting that there is an overall loss of belief in the idea of authority itself. While I was researching my play about the Church of England, *Racing Demon*, which started life at the National Theatre over six years ago, then I was told by a number of inner-city vicars that we lived in what they were happy to call a post-Christian era. The Church was a victim of the general scepticism which characterised the age. It was, you could say, just one more British institution which no longer commanded automatic respect. I was also constantly reassured by the vicars themselves that they were perfectly happy with this state of affairs. Indeed, some of them even welcomed it. Jesus, one South London rector told me, was a friend of the weak, so that if the Church of England itself was in a weakened condition, one might even say this was a good thing rather than a bad one. It helped the Church to a true Christian compassion. Nothing, he assured me, could be more dangerous than a Church triumphant, as in the Victorian age, for that way lay arrogance and complacency. Shuddering with horror when describing the excesses of the American churches of the South, he congratulated himself on the fact that the Church of England with its declining attendances, rotting buildings and half-hearted theology, was mercifully in no danger of being led astray by any vulgar or excessive popularity.

Besides, I was frequently told, even if people did not actually go to church, it was obvious however that they did have some residual spiritual sense. Even those in one parish who never attended the actual services had been distressed when they saw the old church pews out on the pavement waiting to be replaced. They feared something was being lost, even if they themselves never actually went as far as using it. Why should a priest worry if spirituality expressed itself locally by less formal means than weekly attendance at the ever-changing, subtly depressing rituals of the Church of England? At times of disaster people gravitated gratefully towards religious buildings. They still felt instinctively that there was something numinous, something holy about a place where, even if you cannot believe yourself, many people have at least believed before you. Although individuals were no longer willing to subscribe to a code – because we lived in an era where codes were all so hopelessly discredited – they did however continue to wrestle with spiritual problems which brought them, most especially at times of birth, marriage and death, towards a house where they knew these crucial things would be honoured. People, in short, were still religious in spite of themselves.

Once again, I am not sure if I want to buy shares in this popular line of argument. Plainly, only an imbecile would deny that we in the West no longer invest much faith in authority. The reason is dazzlingly simple. In my lifetime, authority has not done much to deserve it. As the author of a matching play about the law, *Murmuring Judges*, I am hardly in a position to deny that a mixture of anger and cynicism now characterises people's attitude, for example, to the criminal justice system. The shocking travesties of justice – most of them racially motivated – which characterised the worst courtroom trials of the 1970s and 80s have not led, in the 90s, to a fitting humility among politicians and the legal profession. Instead we have seen an ever-cruder vindictiveness at the Home Office. Under its current office-holder it has no aim to reform the criminal. It seeks only to slake the bloodlust of *Daily Mail* editorial-writers by doing nothing but punishing him.

As the author of a third play, this time about the Labour Party, *The Absence of War,* I also know that, at least since the election of the present leaderships, nobody has the slightest expectation that a genuine idealism will guide the programmes of the two political parties which have some chance of power. Even the ambition of inspiration is, quite simply, out of fashion. Churchill, significantly a leader at a time of war, was the last Prime Minister about whom the generality of the population entertained overwhelmingly positive feelings. Kennedy, for all his faults, remains the last President. I can also see that when leaders of whatever persuasion attempt to offer even the most hesitant guidelines to suggest a moral basis for citizens' behaviour, they make themselves figures of open hilarity and contempt. At a time when you have been part of a government which chose mendaciously to re-arm Saddam Hussein, when you have been encouraging the leaders of the privatised utilities to risk suffocation by permanent nasal immersions in the public trough, and you are constantly coming upon your own Cabinet Ministers with their trousers wrapped round their ankles, you may well be making a grave tactical error in suggesting that the time has come for the electorate to get Back to Basics.

Yet however dishonest and openly ludicrous the public climate of the time has become, and however deep people's disillusion with their leaders may be, I think this obvious ethos of distrust provides a singularly poor excuse for the frailty of the Church. Why should an institution whose concerns are meant, in part at least, to be not of this earth, feel itself so implicated in the failure of institutions which are? On the contrary, you might expect that at a time when powers temporal are so plainly failing to win the love of the populations of the West, people might very well instead have been drawn towards what was being offered by powers spiritual. If, as it seems, materialism has so sapped Western man that he has reached some sort of dispirited state in which he no longer believes that the best of his dreams and wishes can be embodied in his social ideals, then why on earth is he not turning his attention to a religion which, in theory at least, is supposed to offer some sort of alternative to a life lived purely for money and self-advancement?

But if I cannot accept the professionals' favourite arguments for the decay of organised religion, I am however persuaded by their final line of defence, by what we may call the Church of England's ultimate fall-back position: in other words, that however incoherent our religious beliefs and practices, we are all still aware of the spiritual side of our nature. Plainly, it is true. Asked recently, like Princess Diana, though happily in less publicised circumstances, to attend some open-heart operations, I looked into the deep crimson cavity of the chest, with the red pulsating football at its centre in a lake of blood. The colours were, straight out of the apocalyptic paintings of Fuseli. As I wondered at how we carry around inside us an unseen landscape which so exactly parallels the external world, but daubed in the tones of our dreams, I experienced that familiar giddy sensation of absolute mystery. Who among us actually imagines that the human mind will ever be able to comprehend or 'explain' the universe? When scientists like Stephen Hawking confess such an ambition then clearly they make themselves absurd. The absence in us of any chance finally to comprehend our own existence makes us at every state of our lives prey to intuitions which often appear to us more real than our ordered thoughts. Yet, like many people, I am not sure if the Church of England's present arrangements always play to that sense we all have of the transcendent.

Last year, answering just such an unexplained urge in myself, I ended up alone, driving a hundred miles on a beautiful spring afternoon to visit what is almost my favourite building in England. I do not know if it is true that Oliver Cromwell really did stable his horses in Ely Cathedral, but the idea of it has always summoned up for me an image of almost unbearable power – the rebel army of the republican movement lying down in straw on that massive stone floor, men and animals all night together, with the magnificent twelfth-century pillars soaring above them into the sinister, almost primitive darkness of the vaulted ceiling. As I sped across the pancake-flat fields, I could hardly wait for the sight of that extraordinary, cold, mystic facade. On arrival I cheerfully paid the rather surprising entrance fee, only to go in and find a lot of men in shorts wandering about with walkie-talkies in one hand and drills in the other. There was no chance of peace. Whatever humiliation Cromwell had deliberately inflicted on Ely, it was as nothing compared to the Cathedral's own bizarre decision to allow the *Antiques Roadshow* to be televised there. What are the religious priorities at work when you charge visitors £2.50 to be admitted to one of the most suggestive and hallucinatory church buildings in Europe, only to have the spirit of the place destroyed by BBC carpenters banging away with hammers and by eager townsfolk queuing up to ask whether their granny's chamberpot will turn out to be Delft? It is beyond farce. Yes, the Church's area of expertise is said to be with the spiritual. But at such moments spirituality seems to be the last thing on anyone's mind.

The Christ who threw the moneylenders out of the temple would, I think, have been as bewildered as me by an established Church which has timidly allowed itself to become so close to the secular institutions of the day – the Army, the monarchy, the Government. At first sight, it looks like an organisation which now lacks the missionary courage to set itself apart. It sounds too polite, too frightened to remind us that its determining values are in fact radically different from those of the rest of society. Yet, even as I say this, I am also aware that the very best work of what currently makes up the Church of England is conducted by men and women who barely make mention of those crucial values at all.

Having been brought up in an Anglo-Catholic school which laid great emphasis on daily, somewhat futile reminders to the boys of their own innate sinfulness, I was astonished when researching my play about inner London priesthood thirty years later to meet a supremely dedicated group of men who barely mentioned, let alone spread the Gospel in the regular pursuit of their mission. To point out the most obvious development, they no longer saw conversion as part of their job. Hour after hour, day after day, there they were, out on the street, doing the most menial and demanding kind of work. As they helped young couples to fill in DSS forms, or advised young blacks in trouble with the police, as they visited old people's homes or went to arbitrate in disputes on council estates, they served honourably as society's troubleshooters, doing what was to all intents and purposes social work, and all on half of even a social worker's pay. But at no time did it seem part of their agenda to mention to the people they were helping that every Sunday, in another costume perhaps, they conducted services which related, however loosely, to a much discussed incident in the Middle East two thousand years ago.

Their principal fear, they said, was of what they, in an alarming phrase, called 'stuffing Christ down people's throats'. This, they said, was something which could only 'put people off'. As soon as ordinary people heard what the priests called 'the language of Zion' – all that familiar talk about God and salvation – they were alienated. At bottom, the vicars said, that stuff was unhelpful. It was – another favourite phrase – 'linguistic baggage'. The essential message of Christianity was love. If the priests themselves could express God's love for the world through the work they undertook, it would be sheer arrogance meanwhile to dare to insist to what was now a multi-ethnic community that each member adhere to the priest's own private, culturally determined system of belief.

No one was more typical of this – one might say – defeatist tendency in the modern Church than one compelling South London vicar whose faith was dryer than the driest Martini I have ever tasted. I would say it was ninety-nine parts good work diluted by just one quick twist of doctrine. I asked him for evidence of the power of prayer, in which he said he did unexpectedly believe. Thinking for a while, he cited the example of a very sick child in his parish for whom he had kept an overnight vigil. After twelve hours of sincere pleading with God, the child, whose life had previously been hanging by a thread, had indeed been saved. Impressed by this, I asked him what he would have felt had the child died. 'Oh,' he replied contentedly, 'I'm so surprised when anything happens at all, I don't even notice the occasions when it doesn't.'

Of course this low self-esteem in the modern Church militant made, from my point of view, for wonderful drama. To be frank, I had fun. The play was timely. At that moment the well of public values in Britain was being poisoned by an influential government, itself stacked with millionaires, and therefore self-righteously intent on preaching the virtues of acquisition to others. So it was touching to meet a distinctive body of clerics who were so plainly motivated by concerns other than career or money. But I must admit it was also delightful comedy to come upon a Christian institution which seemed terrified of mentioning its own founder's name. A Labour Party which does not dare use the word 'socialism' is one thing. But a church which does not dare say 'Christ' is quite another. As the century draws to a close in this country, we somehow find ourselves lumbered with both, and in the play I satirised this tendency by making my leading character a vicar who said he always distrusted priests who approached their parishioners 'usually with a lot of talk about Jesus – always a danger sign, in my opinion'.

The experience of meeting these good souls left me confused, because although I liked them so much person-ally – liked them, I suspect, far more than I would ever like their fundamentalist brethren – it did seem to me, as an outsider, that they were perhaps overlooking some essential point about the Christian religion. If Christ did rise from the dead then, call me a fanatic, but I think you probably do have to tell people about it. The inner-city priest's conviction that the poor, for some reason, don't need to be brought up to speed on the news does seem to be vaguely insulting. The Christian faith, after all, is based on the idea of intervention. Mankind is bowling along, following his own sinful ways, and then once and for all – for reasons which his Son then seeks to explain to us, but essentially because God has begun to despair of us – the physical rules of the universe are suspended and God intervenes. I cannot see how if the facts of Christ's life are true, they do not change everything.

It was here, with this most important point, that I began to confront the real implications of my presuming to write a play about the Church. I had embarked on it some-what blithely, assuming that I broadly liked and admired these essentially decent people. To a degree, I thought them ridiculous, but certainly no more so than playwrights – or judges, for that matter. And overall, I wanted to put them before the public as examples of people whose way of life was genuinely valuable. Anyone who comes at the modern world from a different angle has my vote. I also admired G. K. Chesterton's remark that the Bible story is so unlikely that it must be true. Indeed, I regard that as more or less the most convincing defence of Christianity I have ever heard. But then I was disturbed to realise that I was coming to agree with Kierkegaard that Christianity cannot be a 'to some extent' religion. Either it is true or it is not.

But what is it? The more I worked, the more I came to feel that although you may want to believe that Christianity's message may be boiled down to something – however vague – to do with love and its operations in the world, its authority does have to depend on two central claims, which no amount of modernist wriggling can quite dispose of. Christians are people who believe, first, that a man was born of a virgin. And if you ask for a doctor's chitty to excuse you believing even that one, nobody, however, is going to let you off what I think we may insist is the Christian dealbreaker: that a corpse did walk out of a tomb. These two claims seem to me historically to have exerted such a powerful hold over the human imagination that you cannot simply dump them for jetsam at the end of the twentieth century. It is not just that they are part of the ship. Without them, I'm not sure you have any ship at all. More than that, it is positively dishonest to pretend that, if you believe them, then you will not be forced totally to reconstruct the model of the universe which you carry in your head. Intervention is not just one idea like any other. It is a different order of idea.

I suppose what I am saying is that it took the writing of the play *Racing Demon* to make me realise just how profound my quarrel is with the defining myth of Christianity. There were times when I listened to the arguments then raging, for instance, over the question of the ordination of women, and I found I was instinctively against the idea, not on the usual misogynist grounds that Jesus weirdly omitted to designate them for the job, but because I realised that women were in fact the only people likely to bring the unwelcome injection of vitality which would actually keep the whole charade of Christian belief going into the next century. But at other times I felt myself softening, quite simply moved by the palpable sense of goodness that radiates in some churches. If the test of an organisation is its ability to generate individual acts of kindness, then this was a fine organisation.

Those of you who have seen the play will know that I choose to start it with a prayer in which a vicar addresses God on the problematic question of His conspicuous absence from the world. Drawing God's attention to the desperate state of the inner city, the vicar remarks that, at one level, people are resigned to the fact of God's absence. They know that God is going to say nothing. They are used to it. However, after so many years of divine silence, the joke is beginning to wear thin. When God had said 'nothing', they didn't realise he did genuinely mean nothing at all. It is, he remarks, with a mildness characteristic of the Church of England 'just beginning to get some of us down'.

The play kicked off in this manner because it has always astonished me that Christians so often overlook one of the central facts about their God – namely that, in this life, He is nowhere either to be seen or to be heard. What is also peculiar about God's silence – I would even call it eerie – is that biblically it is a fairly recent development. In his book *God: a Biography* the American academic Jack Miles points out that, in the Old Testament, God starts out as someone people can talk to. Or at least He is someone who talks to them. Throughout the early wanderings, the Jewish God is so often in conversation with individual humans that you could go as far as to call Him positively communicative. True, most of what He says is critical. In a paradox which I admit I have never wholly been able to grasp, God is forever communicating His displeasure with creation which has failed to come up to His expectation. He becomes, famously, the master of the rebuke and the lamentation. Yet, after the Book of Job, He grows curiously more and more reticent. It is as if the sufferings of Job seem somehow to break his spirit and He speaks less and less. And in the whole of the New Testament, after sending His Son, He only says one thing, although it is something which even a non-believer finds extraordinarily beautiful: 'This is my beloved Son, in whom I am well pleased.' After this final statement, for the two thousand years which have followed, He is not on record as saying anything at all.

Given this defining feature of God's existence – that He will not, in any terms which you will recognise as being of this world, help you until the day you die with the question of whether He exists or not – then the surprise of those religious surveys which I mentioned at the beginning is not that so few people can articulate their spiritual beliefs but that anyone can at all. As a child, nothing put me off God more than my schoolteachers' highly selective habit of claiming to see Him in whatever suited them – be it in a daffodil or indeed in the abundance of nature. He was there, they said, in the stars. You could even tell He existed by watching the television programmes of David Attenborough. But the appropriation of everything which is good or beautiful or various as evidence of God always struck me even as a child as a particularly dishonest habit. 'When I look out across the fields and see the sun rising, then I know God exists' is a sentiment which has, throughout human history, engendered a quite terrifying quantity of poetry, both good and bad. Buckets of paint have been slapped onto canvas to make the same point. But when you think about it, it is an astonishingly feeble gambit. It can all too easily be countered by equally impressive arguments: 'When I look at a small child, buried at three with cancer, or when I contemplate that famous first charge in the Battle of the Somme, then I know He doesn't.'

For most of us, nothing is more off-putting in the Christian character than its *faux-naif* habit of claiming everything which is conveniently positive and sliding over the things which are negative, or just consigning them to some marked-off philosophical dumping ground called 'the problem of evil'. If everything which is good in the world is to be proffered and celebrated as evidence of God's existence, then what are we to make of the bad? After the recent massacre at Dunblane you were grateful for the fact that no honest churchman even attempted to answer the difficult questions. An agonised Dean of the Cathedral on the television that night made a deeply sincere impression when he admitted that it was impossible to provide any immediate reasoning which could make sense of what had happened, or which could offer any proper consolation to the bereaved. But I am sure the Church equally did itself considerable damage the next morning when it allowed some cocksure vicar on the *Today* programme to go on and piously assert that 'God has a special place for little children.' This kind of certainty – when we all know there is no certainty – is not just deeply offensive, it is perceived by the rest of us as being profoundly anti-humane. It remains for the parents of the murdered children, experiencing a torment which we cannot even begin to understand – and of which the radio vicar most certainly knows nothing – to decide where their children are now, if indeed they are anywhere. If we who do not believe take reasonable care not to trample on the religious feelings of those who profess them sincerely, then why can we honest doubters not ask an equal respect from churchpeople?

It is at moments like these, when the Church does what one character in *Racing Demon* calls 'all that awful claiming you do,' that some of us become positively hostile to

the strategies of religion. For as long as Christian practice is, effectively, social work, we are grateful for it. Our
gratitude has more than a whiff of bad conscience. You
are willing to do work which we are not. You will spend
time with the sick and grieve with the dying. You will try
to heal the wounds which a class of ideological politicians
has created in society at large. But when Christianity
then goes on to the offensive and starts telling us that the
suffering we endure here in this world is somehow justified, that it even has meaning because it is part of an
absent God's larger plan and purpose, then we become
angry. We are angry because we sense a certain unwelcome opportunism in religion which seeks to follow its
own agenda and capitalise on our grief. We do not accept
your view of the world as some sort of divine laboratory
in which we are effectively rats, reacting or failing to
react to religious stimuli. We do not wish to be told in St
Paul's most disgusting metaphor – a metaphor indeed
which reduces human beings even further, to the mere
status of things – that we have no more right to criticise
God than 'the clay has the right to criticise the potter'.

    You will sense from what I am saying how hard I think
it is to find any sense of proper proportion in a life dedicated to propagating the Gospel of Christ. Go too far
in one direction, as perhaps my likeable friends in the
inner city have done, and your tone becomes laughably
apologetic. What Anglicanism's admirers would call
its open-mindedness comes across all too easily as lack
of fundamental conviction. The doctrine of turning
the other cheek seems not just quixotic but downright

disingenuous in the face of the modern world. But head off in the other direction and you pretty soon start to fall victim to practices which violate people's own sense of the privacy of their sufferings. Who, looking at the spectacle of millionaire preachers seeking out cancers among the elderly in California convention halls, or the equally grotesque money-driven antics at Lourdes, can doubt that Christianity is a religion whose power has traditionally depended in part on the almost unique ease with which it can be perverted?

After a while, I came to believe that this disturbing problem of tone, which hamstrings the modern Church and so easily sets one tendency against another, was not a coincidence, but instead actually told you something about Christianity itself. Like some other religions, it has survived precisely because no one can quite say what it is. It was that devout Christian Dorothy Sayers who remarked of the Athanasian Creed that by the time it had informed you that God the Father was incomprehensible, Jesus Christ was incomprehensible, and the Holy Spirit was incomprehensible, you were perfectly justified in concluding that the whole thing was incomprehensible. But who can deny she had a point? So many of Christ's actions and sayings seem to me so deeply ambiguous and so prone to so many different interpretations and conflicting meanings – who for instance can ever understand why on earth He casually blasted that fig tree? What on earth was that about? – that it is hard to resist the conclusion that the durability of the religion bearing his name is down to the fact that it can stretch and bend in almost any direction you choose. (The fig tree, let's remember, was just standing there when He blasted it, and what's more, in just the sort of display of vulgar magic which otherwise He tells us He deliberately disdained.)

Of course it is true that all prophets depend on a certain inscrutability in order to achieve a desirable longevity. As a director friend of mine who longed to be compared to Peter Brook once remarked: 'I'd like to be a guru, but I can't do the silences.' Anyone like me who lived through the would-be student revolutions of the sixties is well used to the idea that the most influential prophets are always the ones whose precise meanings are hardest to discern. In those days, as soon as you said anything definite on the subject of, say, Karl Marx, or indeed about Marxism itself, you would at once be told by some superior soul that you had insufficiently under-stood Marx. Or that your simplistic view of Marx did not take into account some factor or another. Or that if you could read him in the original German you would know that of course he did not say what you thought he did. And of course there was always the most familiar excuse of all, and one which I think may even resonate on these sacred premises: that Marx was not a man whose ideas had been tried and found wanting, but – wait for it – a man whose ideas had never been tried.

However, even by the standards of other charismatic thinkers like Marx and Freud, Jesus Christ was prone to making comments which seem to support an almost infinite variety of exegesis. It was once said that by definition economists could not be expected to get anything right, because, of course, if they did, the world would only need one economist. In some sense, it is not up to a god to explain himself. That is left to the disciples. But a remark like, 'Render therefore unto Caesar the things that are Caesar's, and unto God the things that are God's,' could almost have been produced by computer scientists working at the cutting edge of linguistic theory to formulate the single human sentence responsive to the greatest imaginable number of readings. No sooner does anyone tell you it is quite simple and that they know exactly what it means than someone else pops up to tell you it means the precise opposite. Anyone who heard Margaret Thatcher claim that the Good Samaritan was only empowered to do good because he had first worked hard to amass a considerable private fortune – naturally enough, as anyone who has read the story recalls, by the sweat of his own brow and, specifically, as St Luke is at pains to point out, without any debilitating Palestinian state subsidy – will know that the Bible often seems like some massive, incoherent natural resource, a kind of philosophical building skip full of old planks and plumbing, waiting to be looted for purely private purposes by any old madwoman with a handbag who happens to come along. No wonder it is the book which has traditionally provided so much inspiration to raving loonies in the street.

Is there anything firm, then, we may say about Christian teaching which cannot reasonably be countered by someone anxious to swing the myth round to suit their

own prejudices? Perhaps I am only confirming a few prejudices of my own, but I do not see how anyone claiming
to look objectively at the bulk of the teachings can deny
that this is an anti-materialist religion. At every stage
Christ seems quite clear that our values should not be
determined by our physical needs. What's more, Christ
was incontestably a man who preached the idea that one
day everything will be reversed. Whatever else He was,
He was a man who liked the idea of re-ordering. He
draws me in, as He does many people, when He pro-
pounds the initially attractive idea that eventually – in
whichever world, this or the next one – the first shall be
last and the last shall be first. It is a peculiarly satisfying
prospect. Like everyone else, I become excited at the
thought of that wonderful moment when we're all going
to sit watching those rich bastards bloodying the sides of
their camels in a desperate attempt to force them through
the eyes of needles. One of the funniest sights I have ever
seen on television was the ineffable Lord Hailsham, after
a lifetime of service to the interests of the rich, seeking to
explain to us that Christ didn't really mean it when He
said it would be hard for them to get into heaven. But oh
yes He did. If Christ may be said to speak from anywhere
at all, it is from a platform of redistributive justice. Here
at least is one saying of Christ's which cannot be glossed
out of existence. The meek, whoever they are, will one day
inherit the earth.

But it is when we consider this possibility a little more
closely that our doubts begin to creep in. It is those words
'one day' which stick in our throats. We are living after

all in an age which has been uniquely disfigured by its appetite for violence. As Eric Hobsbawm points out in his history of this century, *The Age of Extremes*, it is sobering now to realise that the infamous pogroms which started the mass migration of Jews out of Russia at the end of the nineteenth century did not claim millions of victims. They did not even claim hundreds. The entire Diaspora, which rightly so shocked the Western world at the time, was triggered by the loss of only dozens of lives. To us, today, sickened and bloodied by the overwhelming statistics of mass murder in our own time, the numbers seem almost trifling.

Since the defining moment of our century, that moment when it became acceptable, even expected, to extend warfare into the civilian populations at home, we have seen an exponential growth in the number of innocent people who have been caught up in wars for which they have not volunteered. If we add together the best estimates we have for those killed in major conflicts this century – the First World War, ten million; the Russian Civil War: ten million; the Russians in the Second World War and after in Stalin's camps: twenty million; the Jews of Europe: six million; China in all wars: twenty million; the rest of us in the Second World War: fifteen million; etcetera – then we arrive at a community of the dead numbering one hundred and ten million. They have died by the violence we inflict on each other. In the shadow of this numbing, overwhelming horror, what meaning does it have to sit and pretend that one day, oh *one day*, everything will be set right?

My own view is that Christianity is declining in the West because, in our hearts, many of us can no longer make any honest sense of it. Its essential message – which is that of justice delayed – seems simply too far off for it to have much impact on us. We have always, perhaps, had trouble with a God who seems to have set life as some sort of insane examination paper which, He tells you, you will pass or fail according to whether you do or do not choose to believe in his existence. But in a century which has been marked out by mass brutality on an un-precedented scale, by the rise of random terrorism, and by the persecution of particular racial and political groups to a degree which almost defies the imagination, it simply seems silly to go on worshipping a God who is repre-sented as telling you that you will finally be rewarded or punished, according to whether you are or are not will-ing to accept the terrifying intangible evidence of His existence. It offends many people's most profound sense of what they feel life to be. Frankly, in the charnel house of the twentieth century, it scarcely matters. What mat-ters is when and how the killing will stop.

In saying this, I have to make clear that I am not sure in my own mind whether Christianity has recovered from the ethical disaster of the Second World War. If it were true that religion has been simply powerless to prevent any of this rise in global suffering, then at least one might regard it as well-meaning but irrelevant. But the evidence is all too plain that in some notorious cases, still unre-solved, it has actively contributed to it. It is hard for us all once more to contemplate the behaviour of Pope Pius

XII, but no one who has ever faced the real facts of how God's representative behaved in relation to the genocide inflicted by Hitler on the Jews can escape the uneasy conclusion that it throws some small light on dangers within Christianity itself.

Even Pope Pius's most passionate defenders will admit that he knew full well what was going on in the death camps of Poland and Germany. He was apprised by independent witnesses, some of whom are still alive today, and who have testified to telling him directly of the scale and horror of what was going on. The decision he then made not to speak out against the massacres, and to advise his Cardinals to maintain a similar silence, remains, by any standard, the greatest blemish on the Christian religion in this century. When he might have warned his flock not to take part in their hideous work, he did not. As one honest German Catholic remarked, 'Each of us has to grope our own way, abandoned and alone.' Yet looking at what is plainly an act of moral madness, we can only understand it when we realise evil is always done by people who believe there is some cause more important than human decency. Here was a man whose actions can only make sense if we judge them by his own dismal criteria – 'Did I save the Church? Did I preserve its power?' – and who actually believed that these criteria should prevail over the ones which really mattered: 'Did I sit in the Vatican and not lift a finger to prevent six million fellow human beings being needlessly slaughtered?'

Pius XII's shocking story is that of a man who put the prosperity of his own Church above that of common humanity. For as long as he believed that the survival of his faith was more important than the survival of ordinary people, he was powerless to help human beings on earth. When he was told of the honourable Dutch Bishops who bravely took the other course and protested to the Germans, he became angry, even deliberately exaggerating the effects of their protests – ninety-two people died, not 40,000 as he pretended – in order to justify his own cowardice. By the most charitable interpretation one may say this was a man who had his priorities skewed. But by any humanist judgement, his 1942 Christmas message marks him as suffering from an evil, an evil in its way as corrosive as that which led to the murder of the Jews in the first place. What are we to make of a Pope who, in the only public reference to the camps in his whole life, could not even bring himself to utter the word 'Jew'?

One might think this a historical aberration of no consequence – no more important, say, than the Inquisition or any one of the religious wars which scarred the Middle Ages, simply the usual story of the wrong man in the wrong place. It might by now, with the passage of time, be thought to have no particular significance. But the disturbing fact is that it was the very intensity of this man's religious faith which led him into his terrible behaviour in the first place. The recent news that people in the Vatican are now lobbying to confer sainthood on the man who did most to discredit Christianity in our age makes you wonder if it is not endemic to this religion – or at least to this form of it – to put the need to prove you are right above the need to prove you are compassionate.

At one level it is amusing that it takes four hundred years for a church to admit that it was in error when it broke the greatest genius of the Renaissance and destroyed his life. But at another level the problems Galileo had with organised religion have not gone away. When these same Cardinals tell gay men that they are in sin when they wear condoms, you are aware that a Church which funked the greatest moral crisis of the century, the extermination of the Jews, is now funking another, the spread of the new plague – and for exactly the same reasons. These are people who truly do believe that there are more important things on earth than our common humanity.

You may think it unfair of me to appear to implicate one church in the crimes of another. Be clear: that is not my intention. What Rome did cannot be Canterbury's fault. But I use this example – the most egregious piece of Christian behaviour in our time, and the aftermath of it – because it illustrates the very thing which worries me most about Christianity. It almost necessarily encourages men and women to take their eye off the ball. No religious statement of the present day has moved me as much as the member of the million-strong congregation who shouted out spontaneously at the present Pope just as he raised the cup for a mass communion in the open air in Nicaragua: 'We asked for bread and you brought us stones.' Many Catholics, in good conscience, now have the integrity to ignore the worst of what comes out of the Vatican. But even so, for myself, I cannot get over the fact that they belong to a universal fellowship whose inevitable and, I think, fatal tendency is to have one eye

on this life and one eye on a second. It is, I am afraid –
and from this stems my fundamental distrust of it – an
essential part of Christianity to believe that our aim is
not towards this life, but towards another. I can only say,
based purely on my own experience, that I do not believe
this is a healthy way to live.

My position, self-evidently, is that of the agnostic. But
I do not, like some agnostics, say 'We do not know'. I go
further. I say 'We cannot know'. And given that we cannot know, we are faced with a choice. Which is more
moral, which is more creative? To live as if we are only
here once and make what sense of things we can? Or is it
better practice to offset all the disappointments and pain
of life by investing our hopes in some sort of eventual get-
out, a moment at which the judgements we have made
on earth will be reversed? Should we live for the moment
when we see other meanings, other values behind the
discernments we have made?

Of course, in asking this I know that all the Christians
I respect believe that their mission is in the here and now,
and that they must have no expectation of any future.
Over and again, they repeat that they must count on
nothing for themselves. Nothing is guaranteed. The best
Christians are the ones who work as if there is no tomor-
row. But I still could not help observing in the months
spent with my vicars that there is a subtle loss of urgency,
a certain psychological softness in the way you approach
life if you subscribe to a religion which teaches you that
there is something else beside life itself. There is a moment
at which your mind drifts upwards. Justice on this earth

seems to matter less to you if justice will one day be delivered in another.

I suppose I cannot help believing agnostics live a life which is tougher and in some sense nobler than yours. Whatever your sincere mutterings about your own short-comings, the fact is, all your money is not on this race. You have a side bet, and that side bet is with someone whose intentions you cannot hope to understand. For us, there is only one life. Judgement is here, either within ourselves or within the hearts of the people we love.

Therefore for us it is bitterly hard. Not for us the con-solation of the famous joke, which I admit does amuse me, even though I know it to be wrong: 'Cheer up, life isn't everything.' We cannot go peacefully to our graves unless we feel at peace with what we have done here and here alone. To you, waste is a necessary fact of existence. It is written into the contract. For us, waste is sin. For you, everything will one day be put right. For us, we must work to make it right now. For you, the way you die scarcely matters for it will seem to be irrelevant under the eye of eternity. For us, eternity has no eye. How we die will be the test of our humanity.

I have spoken here today in the Abbey because, unlike those in what I have called the Christian fall-back posi-tion, I happen to think it a matter of great importance that we do work out exactly what we believe. It is time well spent. I have always had the instinct that even if it does not matter today, it may matter one day – and sooner than we think. The most important fact of my life happened before I was born. In the Second World War millions of people died in defence of a belief, and the sense of squalor and disappointment of the post-war period seems to me inexorably to have stemmed from the feeling that the sacrifice they made has somehow been squandered. I mean no disrespect to Salman Rushdie when I say that his story in the last six years seems to me to be that of someone forced to decide whether they are, indeed, ready to die for their beliefs. When he was first put into a form of effective imprisonment, Salman was seen to thrash around like a man who could not actually believe that he might be killed for the principle of free speech. He issued contradictory statements, said things he later regretted, and generally behaved like someone who was being treated in a way which he found unfair. Yet as the years of captivity have gone on he appears to have found, through his own moral struggle, a form of acceptance – not, goodness knows, an acceptance that he is willing to die, but that if he dies, it will have been for a cause worth dying for. From the moment of that acceptance his stature has only grown. Which of us could have done better?

The one thing that remains to me to do in conclusion is to explain the title of this talk, 'When Shall We Live?' It is part of a pagan saying which – if I may pay an inverted compliment – seems to me to have a force which is almost Biblical. Some of you will know it. It comes from Seneca. Fond, as you might say, of his food and relishing the company of his friends and the prospect of the moments in front of him, he would sit down at table and ask a simple question, just before the dinner was served. This question – a form of grace, let's call it – rings with an historical urgency which is almost pre-Christian, and which one day in some unimaginable future may even justify that strange word 'post-Christian'. Looking at the feast in front of him, Seneca liked to observe: 'When shall we live, if not now?'